SPI
EGE
L&G
RAU

THE COAT ROUTE

THE
COAT ROUTE

CRAFT, LUXURY &
OBSESSION ON THE TRAIL
OF A $50,000 COAT

MEG LUKENS NOONAN

SPIEGEL & GRAU

NEW YORK

Published in the United States by Spiegel & Grau,
an imprint of The Random House Publishing Group,
a division of Random House, Inc., New York.

SPIEGEL & GRAU and Design is a registered trademark
of Random House, Inc.

Library of Congress Cataloging-in-Publication Data

Noonan, Meg Lukens.
The coat route : craft, luxury, and obsession
on the trail of a $50,000 coat / Meg Lukens Noonan.
pages cm
Includes bibliographical references.
ISBN 978-1-4000-6993-4
eBook ISBN 978-0-679-60517-1
1. Luxury. 2. Custom-made clothing. I. Title.
HB841.N66 2013
338.4'768714—dc23   2012042994

Printed in the United States of America on acid-free paper

www.spiegelandgrau.com

2 4 6 8 9 7 5 3 1

First Edition

Book design by Diane Hobbing and Donna Sinisgalli

To my parents

One should either be a work of art, or wear a work of art.

OSCAR WILDE

The woolen-coat . . . is the produce of the joint labor of a great multitude of workmen. The shepherd, the sorter of the wool, the wool-comber or carder, the dyer, the scribbler, the spinner, the weaver, the fuller, the dresser, with many others, must all join their different arts in order to complete even this homely production.

ADAM SMITH

CONTENTS

Introduction   *xiii*

Chapter 1: The Roots   3

Chapter 2: The Fleece   37

Chapter 3: The Lining   67

Chapter 4: The Merchant   97

Chapter 5: The Cloth   123

Chapter 6: The Buttons   145

Chapter 7: The Gold Trimmings   175

Chapter 8: The Tailor   187

Chapter 9: The Coat   219

Epilogue   227

Acknowledgments   235

Notes   239

INTRODUCTION

Not long ago, I came across a website belonging to John H. Cutler, a fourth-generation tailor in Sydney, Australia. The entire site was devoted to one particular overcoat Cutler had made for a longtime client. The coat was, he wrote, "the ultimate expression of the bespoke tailor's art." At the time, I had only a hazy understanding of what "bespoke" meant, though I had noticed the word popping up a lot lately. I had seen ads for bespoke bicycle tours and bespoke spa treatments. Virgin Atlantic airlines, I read, had even begun serving drinks in first class with what were called bespoke ice cubes, crafted in the image of founder Sir Richard Branson. I took it to be a *Masterpiece Theatre*–ish way of saying "customized."

While that is basically true, "bespoke," it turns out, is a much more specific term than that. The word was born in the tailoring trade in seventeenth-century England. When a customer went to his local tailor to order a garment, he would first select and reserve, or "bespeak," a length of fabric. That cloth was then "bespoken" for. "Bespoke" evolved to mean one thing and one thing only: clothing made from scratch, using a pattern drafted to the precise measurements and wishes of one individual.

Four hundred years later, tailors, understandably, think of

"bespoke" as their word. I wasn't surprised to learn that they weren't happy with the businesses that were using the word to inject their products and services with instant upper-crust British cachet. The tailors were also peeved that some apparel makers were advertising their clothing as "bespoke" when it was, at best, only partially made to measure.

On London's Savile Row, the short side street that is the world hub of luxury custom tailoring, a complaint was brought against a company that opened an office there but was making its suits in Germany from only marginally tweaked standard patterns. The petition to stop that firm from calling its wares "bespoke" was rejected by a British advertising-standards regulating board, however, which said that, essentially, the word was too far out of the barn to be reined back in.

Vivaldi's stirring *Stabat Mater* played in the background as I browsed Cutler's website, scrolling through flowery text and clicking on evocative images. There was John Cutler, silver-haired, sixty-something, thick in the middle, with a tape measure around his neck, bent over a worktable. Here were close-ups of buttons and thimbles and pins, lit like still-life tableaux. A shot of a hand pulling a needle and thread through cloth suggested no less than Michelangelo's hand of God. And then there was the coat itself, of course, buttoned onto a tailor's dummy and photographed from every angle.

This was, I gathered, the overcoat to end all overcoats. The garment had taken months from concept to completion, and the tailor had used only the finest materials in the making of it. The coat was made of wool woven from the gossamer fleece of the vicuña, a small llama-like creature found only in the wild on the high plateaus of South America's Andes Mountains. Softer, lighter, warmer, and far more rare than cashmere, it was, the website declared, the world's most magnificent cloth—and its most expensive.

For the lining, Cutler had procured a length of the best Italian silk, created by a renowned Florentine designer. The buttons were the ne plus ultra of fasteners, crafted of Indian water-buffalo horn by a 150-year-old English button-making firm. The coat had even been trimmed inside with an eighteen-karat-gold plaque created by the same master hand engraver who was commissioned by the British royal family to craft a signet ring for Prince Charles and the wedding invitations for Princess Diana.

But that wasn't all. The tailor and his two-man workroom team had made the overcoat entirely by hand, one tiny stitch at a time.

"I made the coat as if machines did not exist," Cutler had written.

This, apparently, was highly unusual even in the bespoke-apparel world. The website didn't come right out and say how much the coat had cost—decorum, and all—but it wasn't hard to click through some links to press coverage to discover the price. The client paid $50,000 for it.

I studied the photographs of the navy-blue overcoat. The plain, boxy, single-breasted number looked, to my untrained eye, like something you might find on Macy's clearance rack. I was stumped. And I had a lot of questions.

Why would someone pay that kind of money for a cloth coat that bore no luxury designer label—no Tom Ford, no Burberry Prorsum, no Loro Piana? A generic, if you will. Where was the fun in owning something that was so under the radar that no one but you and your tailor knew how special it was? Who had the patience to wait weeks, even months, for a coat or a suit when you wanted it today? How did bespoke tailors stay in business in an age of instant gratification and overnight shipping? And just who, in these times of economic turmoil, had a spare $50,000 to spend on a wool overcoat?

I was still thinking about that overcoat a few days later, when I was putting away laundry, trying to jam clothes into my teenage daughters' closets and bureaus, which were already filled to capacity with dresses and tunics and jeans and skirts and sweaters from places like H&M, Target, ASOS, and Forever 21. My closet was in no better shape, overflowing as it was with not-so-great things.

What *was* all of this stuff? I fingered the fabrics and studied the labels. Much of it contained polyester or some subspecies of it—and almost every piece had been made in China. A lot of it looked worse for wear, but that was something I had come to expect. These were clothes with built-in obsolescence. They might as well have had a "use by" date on them, like a container of cottage cheese. When they split at the seams or pilled or went out of fashion, I would, if and when I got around to it, load them into big plastic bags and take them to a local thrift shop, or, if they were really not wearable, just toss them in the trash.

How did this happen? When did clothes become disposable? I know it wasn't this way when I was a kid. Like many of my generation, I grew up shopping with my mother basically twice a year, for spring-summer clothes and fall-winter clothes, mirroring what was, at the time, the traditional two-season cycle of designers and apparel makers. In the late 1980s, globalization started to alter that timetable. Looking for a leg up on the competition, some retailers began to bring in new inventory more frequently. At the same time, a widespread shift of production to China and other developing countries, where labor was cheap and plentiful, allowed apparel makers to reduce prices.

Meanwhile, the design and manufacturing process was speeded up, with instant communication and computerized machinery. Head-spinning turnaround times for products created to meet demand—what manufacturers call JIT, "just in time"—were now possible. Styles that designers saw on runways one week could be in production, as cheap knockoffs, the next. And shoppers, increasingly savvy about trends thanks to the Internet, lined up outside store entrances to get at the fresh goods.

So-called "fast fashion" retailers, like Sweden's H&M, Spain's Zara (which does most of its manufacturing domestically), the United Kingdom's Topshop, and the United States' Forever 21, were brilliant at training us—and especially our daughters—to adapt our shopping patterns to the new normal. What we learned from them, to borrow loosely from Ernest Hemingway, is that there is never any end to shopping.

They also taught us that the clothes we saw in the stores today would likely be gone the next time we came in. New inventory arrives twice a week in Zara's more than seventeen hundred stores, for example. (One study found that the average Zara customer went into the store seventeen times a year—or about every three weeks.) The short life cycle of the stores' collections and the high rate of sell-through means very little merchandise is pushed to sale racks. That strategy keeps profit margins high.

Shoppers learned that snoozing meant losing. There was no time to give serious thought to a purchase—and, really, how much thought was required when it came to buying a pair of $10.80 skinny jeans at Forever 21? Almost no financial or emotional investment was needed to walk out of a store buzzing with the pleasure of having made a purchase. Though the rush was short-lived, the next fix was never far away. And so what if our sweaters bagged or our zippers failed? That just gave us license to buy more stuff.

This hamster-on-a-wheel shopping pattern has serious consequences far beyond causing a lot of us to wish for more closet space. The production of synthetic fibers requires millions of barrels of oil. Conventional cotton-growing relies on huge quantities of pesticides. Workers are exposed to toxins and often subjected to poor factory conditions in the around-the-clock race to feed the fashion beast.

Meanwhile, we are running out of places to dump our castoffs. The Environmental Protection Agency says that Americans discard about thirteen million tons of textiles per year, four times more than we did in 1980, and only about 15 percent of it ends up being recycled. The United Kingdom, which tosses out about a million tons of clothing each year, has a similar rubbish-to-reused ratio. And the mountains of clothing we're building in landfills are mostly made of non-biodegradable, petroleum-based synthetics. The natural materials we toss do decompose, but as they break down they produce methane, a greenhouse gas that's thought to contribute to climate change.

Besides clogging our dumps, depleting resources, and fouling the air and water, the fast-fashion model has helped obscure from view the path that clothing takes from raw material to finished goods. I admit to being unsure if, during the manufacturing process, any human hands ever actually touched the things I'm wearing. I'm probably not alone when I say that I feel as blind to the route most of my clothing has traveled as I once did to the chain of events that landed those pre-formed ground-beef patties in the freezer section of my supermarket. Constant consumption has also distanced us from the idea that the things we purchase are special. The ubiquity of disposable clothing has led many of us to the conclusion that much of what we buy has little value.

That vicuña overcoat on John Cutler's website, on the other hand, was obviously a keeper. It was a *slow* coat—the very antithesis of most of what was being sold in the mall. It got me thinking.

I started reading books about the bespoke world—lovely books, full of black-and-white photographs of elegant people like the Duke of Windsor, Fred Astaire, and Katharine Hepburn. I read about tailors and weavers and shearers and silk screeners, many of whom were struggling to go on. I went down a rabbit hole of history and found that the story of cloth and clothing is, in many ways, the story of man. I studied the suits and coats men wore in movies and on television. I developed a deep sense of nostalgia for something I had never experienced.

And then it occurred to me that what I really wanted to do was go and see all of this for myself. So I emailed and called almost everyone who had a hand in the making of John Cutler's vicuña overcoat and asked them if I could visit. Some of them said okay right away. Others hesitated. Some probably thought I was a little strange. Eventually, they all said yes, and I started packing.

Well, let's be honest. First, I went shopping. Then I started packing.

Plato wrote, "Finally, I went to the craftsmen, for I was conscious of knowing practically nothing, and I knew that I would find that they had knowledge of many fine things. In this I was not mistaken; they knew things I did not know, and to that extent they were wiser than I."

In my travels, I did find wise people. I also found some

obsessive-compulsive types who spent an astonishing amount of time and money curating their own wardrobes. I got to peek behind the velvet curtain into the clubby, little-seen world of bespoke tailoring, where "knowing, not showing" is the unofficial mantra. I met men who share what Tom Wolfe, who knows a thing or two about sharp suits, calls the "secret vice"—men who pride themselves on being able to spot bespoke details, like working cuff buttons and hand-sewn buttonholes, from across a room.

In the company of a renowned researcher, I went high into the Peruvian Andes in search of vicuñas, the skittish, long-necked animals with Kewpie-doll eyes that were almost wiped out by hunters for their valuable fleece and were brought back from near-certain extinction in one of the great conservation success stories of the century. I traveled to Florence to meet Stefano Ricci, the larger-than-life luxury-menswear designer and maestro of silk, who provided Cutler with the overcoat lining. I went to England and watched beautiful worsted cloth come off looms in 150-year-old mills, and saw mottled buffalo-horn buttons being shaped and polished on Victorian-era machines. I ate guinea pig in Lima and truffles in Tuscany.

I watched tailors at work in the basement workshops of Savile Row. I spent time in Sydney with John Cutler, whose personal closet was a museum-worthy collection of handmade sherbet-colored cashmere coats and silk trousers. And I shared some meals with his cast of quirky clients, who, I was relieved to discover, have a sense of humor about their oddball fastidiousness and addiction to bespoke clothing—especially when they are a little drunk on excellent champagne. And I went to see the vicuña coat. I found it draped over the back of a sofa in a penthouse apartment in a Vancouver high-rise.

I discovered a world that is, in many ways, as threatened by extinction as the vicuña was just a few decades ago. Tailors and other traditional tradesmen find it difficult to attract young people into their professions, in part because of limited opportunities for apprenticeships and education, but also because few younger workers are willing to spend years toiling away in an unglamorous back room to become a master in *any* field. European trade-group leaders have speculated, with deep regret, that the current generation of expert artisans—weavers, leather toolers, carvers, shoemakers, and tailors—might very well be the last.

But I also found some who were thriving, against all odds. Having conceded the low and middle markets to the offshore megafactories, they had headed for the high ground of ultraluxury, which was proving itself, again and again, to be an astonishingly resilient niche. In tough times, the wealthiest of the wealthy—like the man who commissioned the vicuña overcoat— had become even more discerning. They demanded top-quality goods, expert craftsmanship, and, especially, things that no one else could have—all hallmarks of bespoke. Savvy manufacturers had also homed in on developing countries where freshly minted millionaires—many of whom were in Mao suits just a decade or two ago—were realizing that they would need to dress the part.

Of course, most people can't afford a $50,000 bespoke vicuña overcoat, or even the $6,000 version made of far more pedestrian sheep's wool, and dropping that kind of money on custom-made clothing might strike some as flat-out obscene. But the fact is that those who can afford such luxuries and choose to spend their money that way are keeping centuries-old trades alive.

I didn't know anything about tailoring when I set out on the coat route. The zenith of my own sewing career was the creation of a calico wraparound three-armhole dress in seventh-grade home-economics class. I came away from my travels in awe of what talented, skilled people can do with fiber and cloth and thread, and envious of the satisfaction they must feel spending their days crafting beautiful things from scratch. They are *makers*, something that fewer and fewer of us can claim to be. And they wish for nothing more than to have the good fortune to be allowed to carry on. I wish that for them, too.

THE COAT ROUTE

CHAPTER 1

The Roots

John Cutler looked up from his cutting table as Keith Lambert walked into his ground-floor tailor shop in the middle of Sydney's high-rise financial district. Lambert, a strapping forty-three-year-old wine-company executive with the symmetrical, square-ish good looks of a TV anchorman, was impeccably dressed, as always. The tailor recognized the navy pin-striped suit Lambert was wearing as one he had made for him a few years back. The fit, Cutler noted with satisfaction, was still splendid. The shirt, too, was a J. H. Cutler creation of the best Sea Island cotton, and the tie—oh yes, he remembered that one—a luminous Stefano Ricci silk in an intricate blue-medallion print. Just right. Cutler greeted Lambert, who, as usual, was holding Rosie, his Jack Russell terrier. Cutler didn't mind. He was used to the dog by now.

The tailor put down his heavy shears and invited Lambert into the consultation room, a clubby space with robin's-egg-blue walls, tufted leather furniture, and an heirloom Persian rug. The paint color had been selected for its serenity and for the way it seemed to help quiet any twinges of doubt felt by clients as they prepared to spend large sums of money on themselves. The cut-grass smell of peony parfum d'ambiance, with which Cutler occasionally spritzed the air when he opened up in the morning, seemed to be soothing as well.

All around, little touches like the framed black-and-white nineteenth-century photographs of the original J. H. Cutler shop, the cylindrical glass case holding old ledgers listing some of his great-grandfather's first orders, and illustrated books, featuring the Duke of Windsor and Cary Grant and other sartorial giants, confirmed for the men who came in to discuss their wardrobe needs that they were part of a glorious tradition. And, in fact, they were. John Cutler was the fourth generation to take up the family trade.

Lambert settled into the green chesterfield sofa, and put the dog down by his feet. Cutler thought his client was looking quite well, despite all he had been through. It was no secret that Lambert had had a difficult stretch. He lost his job as the CEO of Southcorp Limited, one of the largest winemakers in the world, when the board of directors—including Robert Oatley, his own father-in-law and the high-profile billionaire founder of Rosemount Estate wines—sacked him after profits nose-dived. It was the stuff of soap opera, a high-stakes family drama played out in newspapers and on the news. If Lambert didn't talk about it, Cutler, of course, would never ask. There was an understanding between tailor and client; the relationship was not unlike that of doctor and patient, based, above all, on discretion and trust.

Lambert accepted the coffee Cutler offered—it was a bit early for scotch—and told him why he had come. He wanted a new overcoat. He was going to be spending more time in North America and needed something suitable for real winters. For the next hour or so, Cutler teased out Lambert's vision for the garment. Before he suggested a style or fabric, he always tried to understand how his client was feeling and how he hoped to feel when he had the garment on. For Cutler, tailoring wasn't simply a matter of disguising paunches or squaring off round shoulders. Sometimes it was about shoring up a wounded psyche, giving a man renewed confidence to take on the world—whatever the world was throwing at him.

"You fit a man's mind as well as his body," Cutler liked to say. "If you give the wrong suit to the wrong man, you fail as a tailor."

The same, of course, could be said of overcoats. There were so many possibilities—and each one made a different statement. Lambert could go, for instance, with a full-length chesterfield, with its smart velvet collar, but Cutler, knowing Keith as he did, thought that overly formal. The tailor could make him a polo wrap coat, like the kind first worn by British cavalry officers in India to keep warm between polo-match chukkers, but that could come off as a bit rakish—not Lambert's style at all. A duffle, named for the Belgian town that made the heavy wool twill traditionally used for the toggle-closure coat, would be far too sporty; a Raglan, with its diagonal shoulder seams, too slouchy; a British Warm, too military; a car coat, too casual.

Lambert told Cutler that he wanted the fit to be relaxed, but not overly so. He needed something that would travel well. He wanted it to be elegant, unfussy, classic, and with simple lines. Cutler drew some sketches. Lambert made some suggestions. Cutler offered his opinion, and Lambert concurred. After a bit more discussion, it was settled. The coat would be single-breasted, with welted side pockets—and a neck that could be buttoned right to the top to keep out the cold.

Cutler wasn't called on to make many overcoats in Sydney; the climate was too mild. But he was indeed up to the task. He had forty years of experience and a degree from the world's best tailoring academy. Forbes magazine, in fact, had called him one of the best tailors in the world—right up there with the elite of London's famed Savile Row.

I hold that gentleman to be the best-dressed whose dress no one observes.

ANTHONY TROLLOPE

On a rare cloudless October morning in London's West End, I am in a cab, stuck in traffic. The problem is not the standard transit strike or a procession of minor royals or a road race for charity. The holdup today is due to sheep. By decree of His Royal Highness the Prince of Wales, this is British Wool Week, and, to celebrate, Savile Row is hosting a Field Day. The block has been closed to vehicles and turned into a barnyard, complete with a thousand meters of clipped sod, a rough-hewn barn, and two flocks of no doubt puzzled sheep.

When I finally rush into the press reception at Sartoria, the restaurant that is serving as Field Day Central, the welcoming speeches are already under way. I find a spot to stand in the back of the room, elbow to elbow with a sea of men in good wool suits. Most are in dark solids or subtle chalk stripes, but a few have broken out mossy plaids with matching flat caps—the kind of foggy-heath apparel that cries out to be accessorized with hounds. One after another, the speakers sing the praises of wool, farmers, and Prince Charles, who is himself an enthusiastic keeper of sheep.

Ten months had passed since textile executives, designers, carpet makers, and retailers sat on folding chairs in a frigid two-hundred-year-old beamed barn in Cambridgeshire to hear the prince outline his five-year Campaign for Wool, aimed at reviving the Commonwealth's moribund wool business. Charles had kept his double-breasted camel overcoat on as he stood in front of a small podium, backed by bales of hay and a red wagon full of raw wool, and bemoaned the state of the fiber that for centuries had been the glorious engine of England's economy. The cost of shearing sheep, he said, was higher than the price being paid for wool. Demand had fallen, and farmers were reducing or eliminating their flocks.

"The future for this most wonderful fiber is looking very bleak indeed," said the prince, who, following his comments, mingled for a time with attendees but left before the Mutton Renaissance Club served its signature mutton stew.

Committee members, many of whom are in Sartoria this morning, had worked hard since then to coordinate a week's worth of wool promotions and photo ops all over England, designed to remind people that wool was warm, natural, comfortable, and sustainable. Field Day was their marquee event and, it must be said, the one that seemed most likely to have taken shape over a second pour of Laphroaig. ("What's that? Sheep? On Savile Row? Smashing idea, old cod!")

Before dawn this morning, trailers arriving from Devon, in southwest England's moor country, had deposited sixty bathed and fluffed sheep in their temporary pasture. These weren't just any sheep: one group was the U.K.'s last remaining flock of Bowmont sheep, developed by genetics researchers in Scotland in the 1980s by crossing Saxon Merinos with white Shetlands, with the object of producing a hardy, fine-fibered animal; the other was

Exmoor Horn, a stocky, ancient black-nosed breed with elegant backswept horns and a long, dense white fleece. The farmers, too, had been groomed for the occasion. Two historic tailoring houses, Huntsman and Anderson & Sheppard, had outfitted them—and their dogs—in bespoke attire using English wool woven on English looms.

"This is proper cloth," a mill executive is saying to the audience in Sartoria. "It's the cloth that, before Gore-Tex and Polarfleece, a gentleman would put on a tweed jacket with a stout pair of shoes and walk up Everest."

The line gets a laugh, but nostalgia mists across the room as if it had been sprayed from a fine-nozzled hose.

I head outside to see the flocks and to get a feel for Savile Row, the quarter-mile side street that is as meaningful to men who are reverent about handmade clothing as Cooperstown is to baseball fans and St. Andrews is to golfers. A dozen or so of the block's tailors are hosting open houses, and several have scheduled short presentations about some aspect of their business. This is, from what I have read, an extremely rare show of hospitality by a group that, for most of its history, has preferred to keep its activities behind drawn curtains and unmarked closed doors. Open-to-the-street windows, in fact, were unheard of until 1969, when maverick designer Tommy Nutter set up shop with master cutter Edward Sexton at 35a Savile Row, with the partial backing of Peter Brown, the managing director of the Beatles' Apple Corps, whose headquarters were across the street.

Nutter was the darling of mod London. Mick and Bianca Jagger, Twiggy, Elton John, and John Lennon (who, according to the author and historian James Sherwood, was known in the Nutter workrooms by the code name Susan) all sported his signature three-piece suits, with their giant skate-wing lapels, nipped-in waists, and roomy trousers. Every Beatle except George Harrison wore his designs for the *Abbey Road* album cover. As if his designs alone weren't enough to shake up Savile Row's Old Guard, Nutter also dared to show off his wares in provocative window displays—one featured giant purple phallus-shaped candles and another taxidermied rats—created by a young Simon Doonan, who would go on to become the creative director of Barneys. Nutter not only allowed passers-by to see into his mirrored-wall showroom; he also had the audacity to encourage them to come in and browse.

Nutter died in 1992, of complications from AIDS, but if he had lived he probably would have loved the spectacle that is Savile Row today. There are banker types teetering between vexed and amused as they make their way through the crowd; tourists in jeans and windbreakers posing in front of the CAUTION: SHEEP AHEAD sign; buttonhole makers and pressers, up from their basement workrooms, taking extended cigarette breaks; and film crews who can't seem to get enough of Harry Parker, the tweed-clad, apple-cheeked, staff-wielding farmer who appears to be having the time of his life herding his Exmoor Horns from one end of the narrow corral to the other as the cameras roll. And at the top of the street, on a roped-off square of sod, there are several people drinking champagne inside what is apparently an invitation-only sheep trailer, painted a splendid Prussian blue.

Savile Row was developed in the 1730s, on what had been part of the third Earl of Burlington's estate, a large manicured spread on Piccadilly Street in London's then mostly rural West End. As Richard Walker explains in *The Savile Row Story: An Illustrated History*, Lord Burlington was a well-traveled sophisticate and a talented amateur architect who poured an obsession with ancient Rome into the construction of Burlington House, his neo-Palladian palace. Though he had wealth of his own and had married an heiress named Dorothy Savile, his extravagances left him strapped for cash. To raise money, he was forced to develop a chunk of his land. He laid out a handful of streets—Old Burlington, Cork, Clifford, Boyle, and, later, New Burlington and Savile (named for his wife in a bid, perhaps, for redemption after selling off her gardens). Lord Burlington oversaw the building of blocks of town houses, which were soon occupied by aristocrats, military men, and surgeons. Naturally, they needed proper attire, and before long tailors had opened workshops nearby to serve them.

The West End was booming at a time when ideas about how gentlemen should dress were going through a radical change. After the French Revolution, there was widespread rejection of anything that smacked of Louis XVI–style self-indulgence and excess. There was also a surge in appreciation for the classic nude male body, as depicted in ancient Greek sculpture. Meanwhile, the English gentry were discovering the great outdoors, retreating on weekends to country homes, where they spent much of their time foxhunting and dale-walking and pursuing other activities that required unfussy, comfortable attire. When some of these squires wore their country clothes into the city, they helped fuel a desire, even among urban sophisticates, for well-cut apparel made from matte-finish fabrics in subdued colors.

"It happened quickly," Richard Walker wrote. "One moment the average aristocrat was wrapped in velvet and lace and the next he was stepping out in rustic simplicity."

Without the distraction of sheen and sparkle, the focus became the figure of the man himself. Skilled tailors were much in demand. Using shaping techniques and strategically placed padding, they could give almost anyone—pigeon-breasted or pot-bellied—that coveted V-shaped silhouette.

"The perfect man, as conceived by English tailors, was part English country gentleman, part innocent natural Adam, and part naked Apollo," the art historian Anne Hollander wrote in *Sex and Suits*. "Dressed form was now an abstraction of nude form, a new ideal naked man expressed not in bronze or marble but in natural wool, linen and leather."

The poster boy for this neoclassic austerity would soon be a young man named George "Beau" Brummell. The biographer Ian Kelly tells the story of the young man's rise to sartorial legend in *Beau Brummell: The Ultimate Man of Style*. In 1793, the well-proportioned, Eton-educated teenager had a chance encounter with the Prince of Wales, the man who would become King George IV. The prince was so taken with the charismatic Brummell that he arranged a commission for him in his own Tenth Light Dragoons, a cushy regiment whose chief responsibilities were to wear snappy uniforms with tall tasseled boots and to tail the royal as he made his wine-soaked social rounds. Though the prince was twice Brummell's age, he sought the younger man's advice in matters of style and grooming, and Brummell happily dished it out—usually with his trademark shredding wit. The sensitive, chubby prince was said to have cried when Brummell told him that his pants did not fit.

Brummell was promoted to captain but resigned from the military when his regiment was assigned to the wilds of Manchester. Living on a modest inheritance, he occupied himself with maintaining and presenting his dandified self. In his Chesterfield Street home, he often had an audience of admirers—including the prince—who came to watch him go through his daily routine. Brummell advocated cleanliness above all, which in the grime and stink of late-eighteenth-century London was a radical notion. He spent several hours shaving, brushing his teeth, plucking stray hairs, bathing in hot water or milk, and scrubbing himself pink with a stiff brush. (Biographers have suggested that the milk baths may also have soothed sores, which appeared on his skin in the early phases of syphilis.) When his daily toilet was accomplished, he dressed, always with the guiding principle that less was more.

"To be truly elegant," he said, "one should not be noticed."

Brummell's everyday attire was a simple, well-tailored dark-blue wool tailcoat, worn with buff or black breeches and tall black boots (which Brummell liked to say were shined with champagne). He finished off the look with a starched linen cravat, knotted above his high-collared white shirt. Brummell was so exacting that he was known to fling dozens of wrinkled neck cloths to the floor before getting one tied to his satisfaction. When he finally stepped out the door, he was the picture of un-studied elegance and the object of awe. A chance encounter with Beau Brummell could either make your day, if he deigned to greet you, or ruin it, if he mocked your choice of overcoat—or perhaps, worse still, ignored you altogether.

Eventually, Brummell's relentless snarkiness got him into trouble with the sensitive and increasingly pudgy prince. The last straw came in 1813, when Brummell made a crack in public about the prince's weight. "Who's your fat friend?" he said to the prince's companion, within earshot of the royal. (Brummell wasn't the only one who harped on the prince's girth. The essayist Leigh Hunt was imprisoned for two years for, among other things, calling him "a corpulent man of fifty.") Booted from the prince's inner circle, and with gambling debts mounting, Brummell fled

England for France, where he went mad with syphilis, was institutionalized, and died alone in tattered clothes.

Brummell is considered by many to be modern history's first celebrity, as well as the prototype for the public collapse we have come to expect from a certain kind of hot-burning fame. Despite his inelegant end, Brummell's impact was huge. Lord Byron observed that there were three great men of his era—himself, Napoleon, and Beau Brummell—but that, of the three, Brummell was the greatest.

Brummell fascinated Virginia Woolf as well, even if she couldn't quite say why. In a 1925 essay about him, Woolf wrote, "Without a single noble, important or valuable action to his credit he cuts a figure; he stands for a symbol; his ghost walks among us still."

His most obvious legacy can be seen wherever there are men dressed in coats and ties. But he did much more than pave the way for modern business attire. He also helped change the idea of what it meant to be superior in a society that had rigid ideas about class. "His excellence was entirely personal, unsupported by armorial bearings, ancestral halls, vast lands, or even a fixed address," Hollander wrote in *Sex and Suits*.

Brummell's immense fame and influence demonstrated that rank and titles no longer made the man. All that was needed was some serious attitude—and an excellent tailor.

In the footsteps of Mr. Brummell, I set off down the east side of Savile Row, toward the terraced houses built by Lord Burlington, which house the street's oldest tailoring establishments. My first stop is Henry Poole & Co, at No. 15. I know the public is invited inside, but as I push open the heavy door I have the feeling that a firm but terribly polite bouncer will turn me away. Inside, I find Angus Cundey, the hawk-faced chairman of the firm, gamely greeting visitors—even those of us who look as if we may not know the difference between a hacking jacket and a flak jacket. Cundey, a direct descendant of the original Mr. Poole, who started the business in 1806, stands near a low octagonal walnut-and-brass display case filled with silk pocket squares and shiny buttons. Behind him, half-barrel-shaped leather armchairs sit in front of a fireplace flanked by headless mannequins in embroidered military coats and ruffled-front shirts. On one side of the hearth, there is a wall display of black Briggs umbrellas. (The top of the line, a very John Steed number with a whangee bamboo grip, will run you about $500.) Another rack holds a selection of shiny steel swords, available for rent or purchase, should one need to accessorize one's velvet frock coat. Tucked in a corner is a Victorian jockey scale—a leather-seated contraption once used by Poole to discreetly settle disputes with customers who claimed not to have put on any weight since their last fitting.

The walls are covered with ornate frames holding warrants, yellowed with time, certifying that Poole was an official supplier to an international cast of royals, from Emperor Napoleon III to the Maharaja of Cooch Behar. Near the door, a small frame holds a canceled check written out to "Mr. Poole" and signed by Charles Dickens, who died in 1870, still owing the tailor money. Below that is a classic photograph of Winston Churchill wearing a bow tie, a black jacket, and striped pants. Henry Poole made formal-wear for Churchill and many other dignitaries. In fact, as Angus Cundey is scheduled to explain, according to my Savile Row Field Day program, it was Henry Poole who invented the tuxedo.

"In 1865," Cundey says to a group that has gathered around him, "the Prince of Wales was quite fed up with changing every night into a dress coat. He wanted something more informal to wear at Sandringham, the royal family's country estate."

Henry Poole made the prince a short velvet smoking jacket that was, at the time, so daringly casual that it could be worn only within the confines of the country place.

"When a couple from Tuxedo Park, New York—a James and Cora Brown-Potter—was invited in 1886 to spend the weekend at the estate, Mr. Potter inquired what might be appropriate wear. It was suggested he get Henry Poole to make him a dinner jacket like the prince's. So that's what he did. After his visit, Mr. Potter went back to America with the jacket—but without his wife. She stayed behind in England to become an actress. The mind boggles." Cundey pauses for his small audience to contemplate whether the garment was a fair trade for Mrs. Brown-Potter. "At any rate, when Mr. Potter wore his new short dinner jacket back in New York, the Tuxedo Club members and others who saw it were quite taken with it and started ordering their own. Hence the name."

From Henry Poole, I head down the street to Huntsman, at 11 Savile Row. Leaning against a black-scrolled wrought-iron fence is the firm's red Pashley courier bike, with a wicker hamper large enough to hold a new suit; it's still used to make local deliveries. Inside, Peter Smith, the general manager, a large man with floppy brown bangs, is standing near a well-broken-in leather couch set across from a marble fireplace. Two large stag heads, in full antler, are mounted on the wall on either side of the mantel. The room feels like a cross between a private shooting lodge and the lobby of a Nottingham bank. I ask Smith about the heads.

"Ah, yes . . . well," he says, looking delighted to have virgin ears for a story he must have told a thousand times. "In 1921, a customer came in and asked if we could hold on to them while he went to lunch. And he never came back." After six months of waiting, the tailor hung the stag heads on the wall.

It was serendipity for the shop, which by then was well established among royals and the tweedy hunt set as the place to get one's riding garb. Fittings for pinks (scarlet equestrian coats) and patented seamless breeches were done in the back room astride a saddled wooden horse. Huntsman also became known for its use of bold plaid tweeds, woven exclusively for the firm in an ancient mill on Scotland's Isle of Islay, and for its distinctive house style— one-button, sharp-shouldered, with a sculpted waist—borrowed from equestrianwear.

Clark Gable, Spencer Tracy, Gregory Peck, and Rex Harrison were all fans of the distinct cut. In the 1980s, Wall Street traders discovered that the Huntsman silhouette set off their yellow power ties nicely—and didn't mind one bit that the firm was the most expensive tailor on Savile Row. (Sherman McCoy, the protagonist of Tom Wolfe's *The Bonfire of the Vanities*, was a Huntsman guy.) When Ridley Scott was making *Body of Lies*, he went looking for a wardrobe for the character of the debonair Jordanian intelligence chief played by Mark Strong. Huntsman showed him a cache of mid-1990s-era suits ordered and paid for by an Arab billionaire, who had died before he could pick them up. They were perfect.

I head back out on the street, where the tweed-clad shepherds are still urging their sheep up and down the corrals. My next stop is Gieves (that's a hard G, please) & Hawkes, where, according to the Field Day program, a workshop tour is about to begin. The large store, which occupies the corner white Georgian town house at 1 Savile Row—once the headquarters of the Royal Geographical Society—is the result of the merger of two successful tailors: Thomas Hawkes, a cap maker who opened for business in 1771, and James Gieve, who took over a Portsmouth naval outfitter in 1852. Each made his mark with military and expedition garb, and each had a gift for innovation. Gieves, Ltd. patented the Life Saving Waist Coat, which featured a built-in inflatable device and a pocket for brandy, sagely presuming that one would require a drink if one found oneself in the drink. Hawkes & Co. invented the solar topee, a cork-lined pith helmet that became de rigueur Great White Hunter headgear. Henry Morton Stanley was sporting one when he discovered Dr. David Livingstone in Ugogo, Africa.

Andrew Goldberg, Gieves & Hawkes's shiny-bald general manager, is gathering people for the tour. We follow him into the high-ceilinged atrium that had been the Royal Geographical Society's map room and now houses the company's ready-to-wear collection, and then through smaller rooms where pieces from the tailor's archives are on display. There are gold-braid-trimmed Rear Admiral dress coats, RAF tunics, swan-feather-topped helmets, ostrich-plumed busbies, and Captain Bligh–style bicorne hats (Bligh himself was a customer). Glass cases display swords and aviator caps and dog-eared guides intended to help naval officers determine which of their dozen uniforms they should wear when. Among their choices: ball dress, ceremonial-blue undress, mess dress, and tropical mess undress—which, frankly, sounds like the most fun.

Goldberg leads the group single file down a narrow flight of stairs to the workroom, which is bright with natural light from a large window below street level. People on the sidewalk can peer down into the shop to see a dozen tailors at worktables cutting, sewing, and pressing.

"We have one individual concentrating on one aspect of each garment," Goldberg says. "The buttonhole makers make buttonholes. Waistcoat makers sew waistcoats. We have tailors down here who have made garments for the same person for thirty years and have never laid eyes on him."

The tailors don't need to see the customer, because, as in all bespoke establishments, he has been translated into two dimensions via measurements taken upstairs and transferred to paper patterns. Along one wall, I see hundreds of the brown-paper templates hanging from racks, at the ready for the day their owner comes back for a new suit or an overcoat. On each pattern, names are scrawled in black marker. The one closest to me reads "HRH Queen of Tonga." I'm no expert, but even I can see that the queen's pattern implies some serious girth.

Gieves & Hawkes has dressed hundreds of other royals, including King George III and even the King of Pop. Michael Jackson's iconic gold-trimmed military jackets were sewn in this workroom. But most people who have clothes made here—or at the other bespoke tailors'—are not royalty. They are regular men (and some women)—maybe a little paunchy, maybe a little round in the shoulder—who are willing to pay almost any price in order to feel good in their clothes.

"It's really not about the money," Goldberg says. "Money is the trigger mechanism. What they are interested in is getting a suit that fits properly."

I leave Gieves & Hawkes, on my way to Anderson & Sheppard, a tailoring firm that had been a fixture on Savile Row for nearly a century until 2005, when rising rents forced it to relocate to a smaller space on Old Burlington Street, one block away. As I cross the Row and pass the sheep enclosures, I smell warm hay and lanolin, and then, just before rounding the corner onto Burlington Gardens, I smell something else. It is a familiar, if hard-to-identify, scent—rosewood, maybe, with undernotes of fir and

Creamsicle. It triggers memories of being in crowded malls with my two teenage daughters—both giddy with the transformative promise of piqué cotton and distressed denim. Of course, I think, when I make the turn and see clusters of kids in hoodies checking their phones and holding shopping bags adorned with the black-and-white image of a chiseled naked male torso. It is the smell of Abercrombie & Fitch.

When Abercrombie & Fitch, the nineteenth-century American hunting-and-expedition outfitter turned purveyor of sexed-up teen casualwear, announced in 2005 that its first foray off North American soil would be in a nearly three-hundred-year-old mansion on the corner of Savile Row, there was a collective gasp from the longtime tenants of the neighborhood.

"I admit to being horrified," Henry Poole's Angus Cundey told me.

For a year and a half, as the building's 18,000-square-foot interior was revamped to suit its new tenants, Cundey and his colleagues had to walk past a two-story construction wall plastered with the retailer's signature Olympian pecs and abs. The former Queensberry House—later home to a branch of the Bank of England and then a Jil Sander boutique—was a tricky space. The bright lights and white walls of Sander's minimalist showroom had to be scrapped, and the former bank vaults had to be converted into shadowy nooks for T-shirts and jeans. The walls along the grand staircase had to be hung with Mark Beard's giant faux-vintage portraits of half-naked, well-muscled sportsmen, and the twenty-seven-foot-high ceilings, which would have reverbed the A&F house music into aural mud, had to be compensated for with 125 strategically placed speakers. Once the army of beautiful young sales help was hired and the moose heads were hung and the atomizers were primed to pump out Fierce Room Spray, the store's signature vaporous catnip, the store was ready for its March 22, 2007, opening.

Two hundred people stood in the cold rain that day, in a line that snaked down Savile Row. They could probably hear the driving techno beat as they waited their turn to walk through the stone-columned entranceway, past the two shirtless male greeters in faded low-slung jeans who flanked the door. Once they were inside, and had allowed their eyes to adjust to the cavelike darkness, they would be free to fill their arms with $100 polo shirts and $200 jeans. And, for a short time, they would feel that they had been granted membership in an exclusive club where teeth were straight and white, and bodies were toned and depilatoried into sculptural perfection.

The eager customers came the next day, and the next, and the next. Lines for the dressing rooms were sometimes forty-five minutes long. Buoyed by its success in the U.K., Abercrombie, which had reached saturation point in the lackluster American market, would soon build stores in Paris, Madrid, Singapore, Brussels, Copenhagen, Tokyo, Hamburg, Munich, Düsseldorf, Hong Kong, and Milan.

After the initial shock, the tailors of Savile Row tried to look for the upside. The store was certainly bringing new foot traffic to the area. Perhaps, one day, Abercrombie & Fitch customers would be ready to ditch their baggy jeans—and they would know where to go. After all, hadn't Mike Jeffries, Abercrombie's flip-flop-wearing CEO, come to Norton & Sons to be fitted for a bespoke suit?

"People who are going to go into Abercrombie & Fitch aren't going to come in to see us," Barry Tulip, Gieves & Hawkes's design director, told a *British GQ* reporter. "But we do want them to look into the window and say, 'Crikey, that's amazing! As soon as

I've got rid of my hankering for Abercrombie, I'm going to grow up and come to Gieves.' "

I make my way past the groups milling around outside Abercrombie & Fitch and round the corner to Anderson & Sheppard. Inside, a hushed front room glows with an amber light, as if viewed through a glass of sherry. The butternut walls, the parquet floors, the etchings of hounds, the half-shaded wall sconces illuminating the nougat-colored marble fireplace—they are all enough to make me want to lie down on the leather couch, put my feet up, and dive into a book about topiary or tea cozies. On tables near the large-paned front window, ledger books have been left open to pages with handwritten orders from Rudolph Valentino, Marlene Dietrich, Duke Ellington, and Fred Astaire—all devotees of Anderson & Sheppard's easy, soft-shouldered suits.

Down a short hall is a bright sky-lit workroom, where John Hitchcock, the firm's managing director and head cutter, creates what many consider to be the ultimate in bespoke menswear. Ralph Lauren and Tom Ford have both come to watch the trim, dapper tailor at work—and Ford had Hitchcock make him a suit. Alexander McQueen started his career here as a sixteen-year-old apprentice. Prince Charles, Graydon Carter, Fran Lebowitz, and Manolo Blahnik are just some of his more recent customers. I ask him how he feels about having Abercrombie & Fitch as neighbors.

"I popped in once. I thought I should see it," he says. "It's nice, really. Ask any young girl where Savile Row is and now they know. They wouldn't have known a few years ago. They usually have a young man with no shirt on in the door. David and I keep our shirts on, don't we, David?" he says with a laugh to David Walters, the firm's head trimmer, who is on the other side of the room.

Abercrombie is, in many ways, the antithesis of Anderson & Sheppard and the other heritage tailors.

"All of their money is in marketing—merchandising, promotions, advertising, PR—and hardly any is in the product," Anderson & Sheppard's Anda Rowland told me. Rowland is the elegant strawberry-blond former Parfums Christian Dior executive who in 2005 inherited the tailoring business from her tycoon father, Tiny Rowland. "In our case, all of our money is in the product and very little in the marketing."

For most old-school tailors, marketing has always been as alien as sweatpants. Business was built on word of mouth or inheritance; either someone in your club admired your coat and asked who had made it for you or your father took you to his tailor for your first suit and you were expected to mate for life. The closest the tailors came to self-promotion was with their display of framed royal warrants. Even garment labels were seen as being just a tad too show-offy. At Anderson & Sheppard, for example, labels are sewn inside inner pockets, where no one can see them—even if the coat happens to blow open in a gale.

"Those who know, know" is the Savile Row mantra. And there really was no need to shout: Anderson & Sheppard had all the work it could handle.

"In actual fact," Hitchcock said, when he appeared in a BBC documentary, "at one time, we had a problem—we had too much work and we took a salesman on to stop the customers from coming in."

Things, however, were changing. Mass production of apparel, which gathered steam after World War I, continued its growth. A man who wanted a decent suit no longer had to pay a tailor a visit. The Old Guard was aghast. An article on the front page of a monthly leaflet produced by the cloth merchant Dormeuil in

1927 stated the objections succinctly: "He who wishes to be dressed, in the real meaning of the term, must have clothes designed and wrought for him. Nature made individuals; bespoke tailoring assists in retaining individuality. The choice is clear. One may live and die a man. Or, with personality destroyed, the epitaph shall read: He was born a man; he died a 36 regular."

But there was no going back. As mass production ramped up, a shift in style also pulled men away from the sturdy English Cut (and Ivy style, its baggy American fraternity brother) to Italy's new, slinky Continental Look, first made famous by the Rome-based Brioni. A 1955 *Life* magazine article called the appearance in American department stores of Brioni's slim-cut styles "a trap for men" aimed at "outmoding their wardrobes."

Italy became even more dominant in the late seventies and eighties, when Giorgio Armani's fluid, easy-to-toss-on, unstructured jackets were adopted by Hollywood's chin-stubbled elite. The Armani look also bridged "the gap between the anti-Establishment sixties and the money-gathering eighties. It made the wearer seem simultaneously more at ease and more powerful," as Woody Hochswender observed in a 1990 *New York Times* piece about the Italian icon. The Armani suit, he said, was just "right for a new generation of men slipping back into the office routine after a decade of countercultural copping out."

From the informal ease of Armani, it wasn't a huge leap to Casual Friday, which by the late nineties had created a generation of otherwise intelligent men who believed that dressing well meant putting on a clean pair of Dockers. It didn't help that the era's tech tycoons were sartorial duds: Bill Gates was most often seen wearing what *GQ* called the "lazy preppy" look, while the late Steve Jobs made a uniform of Levi's 501 jeans and black Issey

Miyake–designed mock turtlenecks. (Who could have predicted that they would look like Gordon Gekko compared with the world's next digital mogul, Mark Zuckerberg—he of the ubiquitous hoodie?) Personal computers, meanwhile, made it possible to work at home, where there was no reason to ever get out of one's pajamas, let alone put on a coat and tie.

Back in the West End, the tailors were further rattled by the arrival of two young fashion-forward, image-conscious upstarts— Richard James in 1992 and Ozwald Boateng in 1995. Both broke the unwritten codes of Row decorum by cultivating famous clients and seeking out publicity (James ran advertisements in glossy menswear magazines; Boateng staged a catwalk show of his ready-to-wear collection at Paris Fashion Week). Like Tommy Nutter before them, their interpretations of classic English tailoring were presented in jarring color palettes and quirky silhouettes. While the old schoolers were fretting about the young arrivals, they were also surveying their own workrooms and seeing a sea of gray hair. The few younger workers they did have were unlikely to stay more than a year or two. Most were more interested in being famous designers than in being anonymous "makers"—and were unwilling to put in the years it would take to become expert trouser or coat makers. As for the tailors, who could afford to pay a trainee that long, anyway?

Then there was the infuriating hijacking of the term "bespoke." Tailors felt that it was *their* word, and suddenly it was popping up to describe everything from insurance to ice cream. Even worse were the retailers trying to muscle in on the Savile Row cachet by setting up shop in the neighborhood and advertising what they called "bespoke" garments, when what they were actually selling were clothes being made by machines in offshore factories—and then shipped back to London. They weren't necessarily terrible suits, but, the tailors claimed, they most definitely were not Savile Row bespoke.

They decided the time had come to fight back. Led by Mark Henderson, the deputy chairman of Gieves & Hawkes, a core group of tailors banded together in 2004 to form the Savile Row Bespoke Association. They also hired a PR firm—a remarkable step for people whose purpose had always been to draw as little attention to themselves as possible. They registered the trademark "Savile Row Bespoke" and created a label that set out to do for tailored garments what France's terroir-designating *Appelation d'Origine Contrôlée* did for wine and cheese. To be worthy of the label, the garment had to meet the association's strict criteria. Among other things, it would have to be from a shop that offered a choice of more than two thousand fabrics and had an expert cloth consultant on the premises. It also had to be produced with at least fifty hours of handwork and several fittings, made from scratch from an individual pattern created by a master cutter, and sewn by tailors who were based in England.

To address the skills gap and the aging of the tradesmen, the group launched an apprenticeship scheme designed to get young people to take up the tape measures and shears. They inaugurated a bespoke tailoring course in association with a local college, upon completion of which students could apply for an SRBA-funded apprenticeship on Savile Row. They also appealed to the local government to acknowledge Savile Row as a national treasure worthy of special zoning laws.

"We're one hundred yards off Bond Street, which is the most expensive retail space in the world," Henderson told me. "And we had working tailors in our basements. We had to figure out a way to stop development." After a lengthy study, the Westminster

Council concluded that Savile Row should be designated a Special Policy area, which meant that workshop space would be protected for the use of tailors only.

An attempt to legally reclaim the word "bespoke" was less successful. A disgruntled customer brought a complaint to the British Advertising Standards Authority against a Swiss-owned company called Sartoriani, which had set up a small office and showroom in the basement at 10 Savile Row. Sartoriani advertised "bespoke" suits, "uniquely made according to your personal measurements and specifications"—at one-fourth the price of a suit from a traditional tailor. While customers were, in fact, having their measurements taken on Savile Row, the garments were being machine-cut and sewn in Germany. (Sartoriani never claimed otherwise.) Not fair, the complaint said—and certainly not "bespoke." The ASA, however, sided with Sartoriani. To most people, it said, "bespoke" had simply come to mean "made for you." It didn't matter whether it was a $5,000 suit made by hand on Savile Row or a $400 suit made by a robot in China.

"You are looking at the difference between a fine painting and a print," a disappointed Henderson told a reporter after the ruling.

The word "bespoke," at the same time, was well on its way to becoming a buzzword used by all kinds of businesses. Suddenly, there were bespoke salad bars, bespoke investment groups, bespoke bicycles, bespoke walking tours, bespoke cupcakes, bespoke headphones, bespoke headboards, bespoke toilet seats—even something called Bespoke Hair Artisans, which managed to incorporate not one but two trendy words into its name when it opened its doors in Edina, Minnesota. Looking at the popularity of the term, a May 2012 *Wall Street Journal* article noted that the U.S. Patent and Trademark Office listed thirty-nine active applications and registrations that used the word "bespoke." Perhaps some of the applicants had relied on consultants offering bespoke patent strategies.

True bespoke tailors were also struggling with the new phenomenon of "mass custom" production, which used technology, and cheap labor, to bring made-for-you suits to the masses. On Madison Avenue, a company called My Suit, owned by the South Korean conglomerate BK House, opened a flagship store and launched a website on which customers could design their own suit for less than $1,000. The company's Mexican factory, capable of producing one million suits a year, could turn a made-to-measure order around in two weeks.

"It's like Build-A-Bear for grown men," James Hancock, the vice president of sales, told *Women's Wear Daily*.

Indochino.com, launched by two Canadians in Vancouver, called itself the "fast fashion" option for custom menswear. Its suits are produced in a Shanghai factory, based on measurements that customers take themselves and submit online. There was no middleman and no storefront.

Of course, getting a decent fit assumes that the customer knows how to use a tape measure on himself—something that is not easy. New technology appeared that aimed to take the human error out of measurements. Body scanners, using technology borrowed from gaming and security-screening technology, popped up in traditional retailers like Brooks Brothers in Manhattan and at upstarts like Tailor Made London. The scanners could produce almost instant digital body maps.

Tailor Made's website acknowledged that what it was peddling wasn't equal to a Savile Row experience or product: "Nothing can surpass the touch, the look, or the feel of bespoke suits, but who really has the time for ponderous measuring sessions and multiple fittings these days? It's only a bespoke suit after all."

Meanwhile, software developers were racing to perfect a system that would use personal computer cameras to create a body map in the privacy of one's own home.

To make clear the distinctions between these cut-rate mass-custom producers and their own handmade goods, the tailors knew they had to do a much better job of telling their story. They launched websites, took on marketing consultants—even started blogging and tweeting. Their mission was to recast themselves as luxury brands and to distance themselves from the widely held belief that their industry, however charming, was dying.

It was their good fortune that the qualities that made them special—their devotion to craftsmanship, their use of sustainable materials, their focus on provenance, their ability to customize, their supply-chain traceability, their very *slowness*—had become selling points in the mid- and post-recession years for a wide variety of products. J. Crew posted videos of Italian leatherworkers making shoes for the American brand on its website and began identifying some of the mills that produced its fabrics for garments featured in its catalogs. Restoration Hardware raised prices and filled its catalog with handmade lamps and tables, accompanied by lush photo spreads of artisans pounding iron and shaping wood, betting on the appeal of craftsmanship. West Elm, another furniture retailer, teamed up with Etsy, a website for vendors of handmade and one-of-a-kind products. Patagonia introduced the Footprint Chronicles, which allows consumers to track the making of, say, a down jacket from a Hungarian duck to a Reno, Nevada, warehouse. Marks & Spencer, the London department store, announced a traceability project called String that would track every item of clothing it sold from raw material to finished product.

At the same time, European luxury brands that were founded on craft, as most were, shifted their advertising focus to reflect their handmade pedigree. Gucci launched a traveling Artisan Corner, in which Florentine leatherworkers set up a small work-shop in a Gucci store to assemble and finish handbags in front of spectators. A year later, Hermès would conduct a similar work-shop tour, bringing a troupe of leatherworkers and silk screeners to select stores all over the world.

The global spread of luxury products, meanwhile, also spurred a desire for the custom-made and the one-of-a-kind. Peo-ple with money to spend were searching for something special that would distinguish them from the increasingly ubiquitous luxury brands.

"Mass luxury is not luxury at all, because anyone can buy it; it's available everywhere and produced in enormous quantities. Real luxury is about scarcity," Patrick Grant, the director of Nor-ton & Sons, a Savile Row tailoring firm, said in an interview in the *South China Morning Post*.

Even in China, where luxury products are a relatively new concept, discerning shoppers were starting to turn away from la-bels in search of personalized goods and services with a compel-ling story behind them—preferably one that was told in a posh British accent. In a fever of Anglophilia, the Chinese were em-bracing anything that conveyed good breeding and connoisseur-ship, including polo (which had last been popular in China about seven hundred years ago), cricket, golf, croquet, scotch whiskey, Jaguar automobiles, Victorian oak sideboards, boarding schools—and bespoke.

And they were descending on the U.K. and Europe to shop.

In 2010, the London Luxury Quarter, a consortium of three hundred high-end shops in the West End, including Savile Row, reported that Chinese tourists were spending almost $1,000 whenever they made a purchase—up 155 percent from the previous year. Increasingly sophisticated and knowledgeable Chinese shoppers poured about $470 million into the U.K. economy that year, ten times more than they spent in 2007. Visa applications by Chinese rose by 40 percent—and were expected to surge if, as retailers urged, the government simplified the ten-page application. Harrods and Selfridges both saw double-digit increases in sales to Chinese tourists when they began accepting UnionPay, the Chinese credit card, and added a Mandarin-speaking sales staff. Burberry, the British fashion house, reported that, in 2010, 30 percent of sales in its U.K. stores were to Chinese customers. A company called London Luxury introduced private-car shopping tours to bespoke tailors led by a Mandarin-speaking guide. For an extra $425, customers could go down into the basement to watch the tailors at work. Hilton Hotels launched a Chinese welcome service in four London hotels, providing Chinese-speaking staff, traditional Chinese breakfast food, and in-room Chinese TV, tea, and slippers. Global Blue, a retail-market-research firm, found in a study of Chinese tourists who had come to Europe to shop that many of them were unhappy that they had been unable to spend all their money in the time they had available.

The Chinese were going on another kind of buying spree in the U.K. By 2012, Chinese companies would own Aquascutum, Gieves & Hawkes, MG Rover, the Birmingham City Football Club, and Weetabix, the quintessentially British breakfast cereal.

Savile Row tailors didn't like much of what was happening around them, but they did find reasons to be optimistic. A year after my first visit, in 2010, two hundred students went through the pre-apprenticeship course at Newham College; thirty of the best were working alongside master tailors as official Savile Row Bespoke Association trainees. There was also a surge in the popularity of trunk shows, in which tailors traveled to the United States and beyond to hold fittings in hotels. Tailors reported that their customers were getting younger—and they were arriving full of knowledge and opinions derived from studying websites and watching episodes of *Mad Men*.

Meanwhile, higher labor, materials, and freight costs in Asia, coupled with a general backlash against outsourcing, was spurring a renewed interest in closer-to-home manufacturing and locally sourced raw materials, both in Great Britain and in the United States.

Prince William married Kate Middleton, and in so doing shined a light on the sartorial traditions of Old England. (Among the viewing audience were an estimated thirty million Chinese.) Savile Row tailors reported a rush of orders from men who made the guest list. Business on Savile Row grew by 10 percent, even as the world's economy faltered. Wool prices in Australia rose to record highs. And the venerable Gieves & Hawkes undertook a major renovation to transform itself into a men's emporium, showcasing several niche businesses under its roof.

Among the shops-within-the-shop were a branch of Bentley's, a London dealer in vintage steamer trunks and 1920s cocktail shakers; a salon called Gentlemen's Tonic, which specializes in classic wet shaves; Carréducker, a hip husband-and-wife team of custom shoemakers who could be seen working in a glass booth surrounded by hand-shaped lasts; and a shoe-shine station operated by a young man named Justin FitzPatrick, an expert in military-grade polishing and a well-known blogger among footwear fanatics called the Shoe Snob. Gieves & Hawkes set out to be more than a store. It wanted to be an experience, as alluring to a certain kind of man as its upstart American neighbor, Abercrombie & Fitch, was to its younger and scruffier, but no less loyal, clientele.

I leave Anderson & Sheppard, pass by Abercrombie & Fitch again, and arrive back on Savile Row, in front of the sheep trailer, where there are a dozen or so people with champagne flutes in their hands. A young security guard in a waxed-cotton field jacket and Wellington boots shifts his weight from one leg to the other, his vigilance apparently on the wane. Behind the split-rail fence, the poker-faced sheep are chewing on hay.

Most of the street is in shadow, but the late-afternoon sun has lit up the white façade of Gieves & Hawkes and illuminated the small-leafed ivy curling out of planters and around the black iron rods of the fence, the navy window awning with the forthright white lettering, the arched entranceway over the black wooden double doors, and, above them, the Union Jack, moving a little in a weak breeze. I walk down the west side of the street, past Ben Sherman and Lanvin, to Ozwald Boateng, the large shop at the corner of Savile Row and Clifford, in the space once occupied by Anderson & Sheppard. I peer through the windows into the gallery-like store. Along one wall there is floor-to-ceiling shelving, painted a glossy black, and in each lighted opening there are men's shirts, folded flat and arranged by intensity of color—celery to fern, sky to indigo, petal to poppy. In the shop window, I catch a reflection of myself. My sweater, which I had thought fashionably oversized, is, I see now, overwhelming. My slim pants have gone baggy at the knee.

I decide to do one more lap of Savile Row, before the sheep are loaded back into their trailers, before the old Victorian doors are locked, before the street returns to what it was yesterday and what it will be tomorrow. I stop first in a small exhibit barn, erected for Field Day, where tables hold the lovely, simple equation of wool—raw fleece, skeins of twisted yarn, bolts of cloth. Then I'm in front of Huntsman again, looking down over its wrought-iron fence to the basement workroom. Two tailors, older gentlemen with bald heads, are sitting near the big front window, which, even though it is below street level, lets in plenty of light. One, in a lavender shirt, has a garment in front of him on a work-table, and the other, in a dark vest and a white shirt, has his project on his lap. Their heads are bent, and for a moment each has his right hand poised at the top of the stitch, like conductors about to cue the orchestra.

On the sidewalk, a young man with a trimmed brown beard and tortoiseshell glasses is striding toward me. He is wearing what I am almost certain is a bespoke suit. It is a bold gray-and-black Prince of Wales check, and he has paired it with a maroon-and-white pinstriped shirt and a dark silk tie. On his feet are black brogues, polished to an obsidian sheen. I realize that I am envious of this man in his beautiful suit, of all the men in their suits.

I'm envious of the excitement they must have felt when they walked into their tailor of choice, knowing they would be placing an order. I'm envious of the time they spent paging through books of cloth, weighing the merits of this nubby gray or that rich navy. I'm envious of the thrill they must have felt when their tailor held their new jacket behind them and they reached back and slipped their arms into the sleeves and felt it settle onto their shoulders, perfectly flush to their neck. And I'm envious of the moment, that delicious moment, when they fastened the buttons for the first time, gave the lapels a sharp little tug and saw, yes, that it fit, just right.

CHAPTER 2

The Fleece

A few days after his first consultation about the coat, Keith Lambert returned to John Cutler's shop to discuss fabrics. The tailor was not surprised to hear his client say that he was thinking cashmere—Keith always wanted the very best. John showed him books of swatches—in the tailoring trade they're known as "bunches"—and Keith rubbed the small squares of sample cloth between his fingers. Then John had a thought. He hesitated. Perhaps . . .

"We could do cashmere, Keith," he finally said. "Or we could take it a step further. . . ."

John got up and walked into a back room. A few minutes later, he reappeared holding a long, narrow mint-green cardboard box, embossed on top with a gold coat of arms and the words "Dormeuil. The World's Best Cloths." John placed the box on the table in front of Keith, then lifted the lid and took out a bolt of folded dark-blue cloth. He laid the fabric across his client's lap.

"Feel that," he said.

Keith touched the edge of the material, then ran his hand along the length of it. John knew just what he was feeling. The cloth was unimaginably soft—softer than the finest cashmere, but with more substance and spring—and it had a short, distinct nap that begged to be stroked.

"That's lovely," Keith said. "What is it?"

"Vicuña," John said, almost whispering the word. "Very rare. From Peru."

John watched Keith caress the fabric and study the play of light and shadow in its shallow folds. For twenty years, the tailor had been holding on to this extraordinary and, at $6,000 a yard, staggeringly expensive cloth, waiting for the right client. Yes. He could see it now in Keith's face. He had found him.

What is this strange animal who lives high above the clouds in a region where practically no other mammals can survive; this small creature who, inconsequential in stature and number, because of its almost priceless pelt, has been singled out from among the animals of the earth?

SYLVAN STROOCK

Jane Wheeler hates winter in Lima. From May to November, a dense, cool ocean fog, known as the *garua*, enshrouds the sprawling Peruvian city of nine million in a depressing, damp all-day dusk.

"Another beautiful day," the owlish sixty-seven-year-old scientist with cropped graying hair says from behind the wheel of her black pickup. It is a murky morning in late July 2010, and we are heading for her office at the University of San Marcos.

I had arrived in Lima after midnight and been driven to Jane's home about twenty miles south of the city. From the back of the taxi, I had been aware of the fog, the way it softened the lights on the hills and fuzzed the headlights of oncoming trucks. It made the trip dreamlike and thrilling. I was in the land of the Incas, Pizarro's City of Kings, heading down the Pan-American Highway on the ragged desert edge of South America. But in the morning gloom, from the passenger side of Wheeler's Toyota, I see that, for all its exoticism and glories, Lima is, above all, a place that cannot afford bad lighting.

The ash-gray towers of the Cementos Lima factory look like a haunted dust-bowl Oz. Shantytowns of woven reed, scrap tin, and cardboard cover the sand hills on the metropolis's outskirts. In the city itself, grime seems spackled to every surface, from the crumbling adobe tenements to the decaying colonial mansions. And then there is the traffic: a junkyard honkfest of crowded buses, top-heavy trucks, and backfiring jalopies trailing black exhaust while slaloming around pedestrians, who are, literally and quite necessarily, running for their lives. I am not surprised to find out later that Lima has one of the highest rates of pedestrian fatalities in the world.

Jane has been making this commute for most of the past sixteen years. The Washington, D.C., native is an archaeozoologist—an analyzer of animal remains found at archaeological sites. She holds degrees from American University, Cambridge University, and the University of Michigan, and she did postdoctoral work at the University of Paris. Her field studies have taken her from Mexico to Scotland to Iran, but it was in Peru that she got famous—not Dian Fossey or Jane Goodall famous, but renowned in the international community of people who care about South American camelids: llamas, alpacas, guanacos, and, the reason I was here, vicuñas. Jane was going into the mountains to observe them in the next few days and had agreed to let me tag along.

A guard waves us through a security gate at the university, and Jane parks under a lone palm tree in front of her office building, a concrete bungalow that looks more like a restroom at a city park than like a world-class research center. Before walking through the office door, I read out loud, in fractured Spanish, the words on a brass sign. UNIDAD DE VIROLOGIA Y GENETICA MOLECULAR.

"Except it's not called that anymore," Jane says, without further explanation. Inside, the office is divided in two: her veterinarian husband, Raul Rosadio, and several grad students on one side of a wall, Jane on the other. Besides being a university office and lab, this is also headquarters for CONOPA, a Peruvian nonprofit organization run by Jane and Raul that is dedicated to camelid research and conservation, and to improving the well-being of the herders who depend on the animals for survival.

Jane's office is lined with file cabinets and bookshelves. On top of one cabinet, a clear plastic bin holds bleached bones. Next to that, a cardboard carton that once apparently carried boxes of Angel breakfast cereal has the word "Vicuña" scrawled across it in black marker. Jane offers me a straight-backed chair in front of her desk and tells me that I'm welcome to browse her collection of books, journals, and papers about vicuñas—many of which she has written herself.

"Most people who come really just want at the library," she says and turns her attention to her large computer monitor.

I stack up a pile of material and start reading. Vicuñas, distant relatives of Arabian dromedaries and Bactrian camels, are found only on the Andes altiplano, the desolate windy plateau between twelve thousand and sixteen thousand feet that stretches from southern Peru to northern Argentina. At those elevations, oxygen levels are low and temperatures are often well below freezing, but, more than any other mammal, vicuñas are built to handle extremes. Relatively large hearts and an unusually high number of red blood cells allow them to make efficient use of limited oxygen. Lower incisors that grow constantly let them gnaw on the toughest alpine grasses without wearing down their teeth. Cushioned hooves stand up to rocky terrain, and long necks make it possible for them to spot predators from a distance. Extra-rich milk allows nursing babies to mature quickly.

Most remarkable, though, is their fluffy cinnamon-colored coat, which provides protection from the intense high-altitude sun and insulation from the cold. It is made up of individual fibers that are a minute 12 microns (1/25,000 of an inch) in diameter, finer than cashmere, which averages about 19 microns. Human hair, by contrast, ranges from about 40 to 120 microns.

If the vicuñas' adaptation to their difficult habitat is Darwinian, their appearance leans more toward the Disneyesque. Vicuñas seem conjured up by a team of Imagineers who were pressed by their bosses to come up with something *really* cute this time. Sleek wedge-shaped heads top their elegant long necks. Split upper lips, a camel-family trait, help fix their dark mouths in pursed half-grins. Large black eyes, outlined pharaoh style, are trimmed, almost inevitably, with a thick fringe of über-Bambi lashes. The overall effect: heart-yanking vulnerability meets big-screen charisma.

Inca societies revered the vicuñas as livestock of the gods and had strict rules governing the use of their fleece. Only royalty was allowed to wear vicuña garments or sleep on vicuña bedclothes—and violators had to answer to what may have been history's first fashion police. The punishment was no joke: unauthorized wearing of vicuña was grounds for execution.

The production of the fibers was also tightly controlled. In order to allow the animal's coat to reach full growth, shearing took place in designated regions only every three or four years, during a highly ritualized communal roundup called the *chaccu*. On a day selected by the Incan king, thousands of men would walk out across the puna and form a human chain surrounding huge herds of vicuña. Moving forward in an ever-tightening circle, the Indians drove the animals into makeshift corrals, then clipped and released them. Vicuñas produce just under one pound of fleece per shearing—and grow it back slowly, at the rate of about an inch a year. The fibers are quite short, which makes spinning difficult.

That job, in Inca times, fell to the *aclla*, or Virgins of the Sun, young girls who were selected as much for their beauty as for their dexterity to be the spinners and weavers to the royal family. Isolated in a special building, they were kept busy by the nobles, who, by some accounts, had the capriciousness of fourteen-year-old girls, often changing outfits several times a day and wearing each garment only once. Cloth was treated like gold and tucked away in imperial warehouses.

In 1532, when Francisco Pizarro and his small army of about 160 men arrived on Peru's northwest coast, there were an estimated two million vicuñas on the Andean altiplano. But the conquistadors, who had brought horses, long-barreled guns, and no spiritual attachment to the odd, long-necked animals, quickly began to reduce the herds.

As early as 1553, the conquistador Pedro Cieza de León wrote, "In bygone times, before the Spaniards conquered this kingdom, there were throughout these sierras and countryside great numbers of llamas, and even guanacos and vicuñas. But the Spaniards killed them off so fast that there are almost none."

Garcilaso de la Vega, the son of a conquistador and an Incan princess, echoed that observation in his account of the history of Peru, published in the early seventeenth century: "Such in those times was the abundance of their Game but now it is said, that such havock hath been made by the Guns which the *Spaniards* use, that there is scarce a . . . *vicuña* to be found but what are affrighted into the Mountains, and inaccessible places, where no path or way can be made."

Once vicuña blankets were sent back to Spain for the bed of King Philip II, the animals' fate was sealed. A desire for this New World Silk, as it was called, swept Europe. For the next several hundred years, the slaughter continued at a breathtaking pace. Some people did notice that the great herds were dwindling and spoke out about it. In 1768, viceroy Marqués de Rocafuerte sounded an alarm and said, "Whoever should find the vicuñas may shear them but on no account kill them, so that the species shall not become extinct."

The notion that an entire species might disappear was a radical one at the time. Simón Bolívar, Peru's forward-thinking first governor after the country won independence from Spain, however, believed wholeheartedly that, where the vicuña was concerned, extinction was a real threat. In 1825, he declared a ban on vicuña hunting and laid out strict guidelines governing when live shearing could take place. Shipping records show that between 1663 and 1853 the skins of 1.5 million vicuñas were supplied to European markets for vicuña gloves, shawls, hats, and cloaks. In a 1901 newspaper ad, a Bryan, Ohio, department store touted vicuña underwear as the perfect choice for men who were "rheumatical sufferers." The drawers, they claimed, were "worth their weight in gold." Each pair cost a dollar.

In 1920, trade in vicuña products was forbidden. Six years later, the exporting of vicuña fiber was outlawed. A law prohibiting the hunting of vicuña, guanaco, and chinchilla was passed in 1940. None of the forty-odd other attempts to legislate the conservation of the species had any effect, since they failed to include a specific plan for enforcement and were not coordinated with Argentina, Bolivia, or Chile, each of which had a vicuña population.

By the time vicuña fever hit America, it was accepted as fact that fleece could be harvested only from dead animals. That point was made in a flowery little book called *Vicuna: The World's Finest Fabric*, produced in 1937 by Sylvan Stroock, the owner of S. Stroock & Co., a prominent New York textile manufacturer who specialized in vicuña and other rare cloth: "Yes, rare indeed is the vicuna, that curious little animal which must give up its life to furnish the hair for the richest and most luxurious fabric that has ever come from the loom."

Forty animals were required to make one overcoat, more if the cloth was a heftier weave. At Christmastime in 1938, shoppers crowded around the window of Marty Walker, a Manhattan menswear store, to see a special-edition heavyweight Stroock vicuña coat that was selling for $900 and was advertised as being made from the pelts of sixty animals.

By the mid-twentieth century in America, nothing said panache like a vicuña overcoat. Desi Arnaz, Marlene Dietrich, Greta Garbo, Leonard Bernstein, Groucho Marx, Nat King Cole, Sammy Davis, Jr., Lena Horne, and Dean Martin all had one. Vicuña also came to symbolize a certain kind of moral decay, thanks to its role in Billy Wilder's 1950 classic, *Sunset Boulevard*. In one of the film's most memorable scenes, a sneering menswear salesman hisses into the ear of William Holden's kept-man character, "As long as the lady is paying for it, why not take the vicuña?"

Neiman Marcus, the Dallas emporium of extravagance, became closely identified with the fabric. While a New York store might have two or three coats in stock, Neiman Marcus kept an inventory of three hundred, in a full range of sizes, priced at $695 each. Stanley Marcus, the former chairman of the board, recalled in his memoir, *Minding the Store*, the day he got a call from an Egyptian man who was in New York shopping for vicuña coats for his entire family but hadn't been able to find a store that could accommodate them. Neiman Marcus had plenty of coats, Marcus assured the man, who promptly flew his entire family to Dallas to get five vicuña coats: one for himself, his wife, his daughter, and his two sons. After he made the purchase, they all flew back to New York.

In 1955, *Life* magazine reported on a "melee of elegance" among Seventh Avenue garment makers, who were being swamped with orders for clothing made of luxury fabrics. One manufacturer of $10,000 mink-lined vicuña coats told a reporter that he was afraid he would run out of vicuña before he ran out of customers.

In 1957, Jack Kerouac wore an oversized vicuña coat that came down to his ankles to a brunch with Salvador Dalí at the St. Regis, according to the biographer Ellis Amburn. The coat had been given to Kerouac by a friend, who had stolen it. Kerouac later traded it to the poet Randall Jarrell for a fur-collared leather bomber jacket. That same year, the slugger Ted Williams ended up with one by force majeure, according to a tale told to a reporter at the *San Francisco Chronicle* by a salesclerk. An earthquake had struck while Williams was trying on a vicuña coat on the fourth floor of Roos/Atkins, a Sutter Street menswear shop, and he had dashed in fright out of the store wearing the coat. The clerk said he had not returned.

A year later, a political scandal turned vicuña into a household word. Sherman Adams, Dwight Eisenhower's White House chief of staff and a former governor of New Hampshire, was forced to resign when it was revealed in House subcommittee hearings that he had accepted a vicuña overcoat from Bernard Goldfine, a Boston textile manufacturer who was being investigated for Federal Trade Commission violations.

Vicuña hung in windows of Arabian palaces and was draped over sofas in the Kennedy White House. Newspapers noted that Hedy Lamarr wore a vicuña coat to her 1966 Florida court date to plead innocent to shoplifting $86 worth of merchandise. The tawny overcoats were de rigueur for everyone from Italian mafiosi to Japanese dentists.

Vicuña, it seemed, was everywhere. And then the supply all but dried up. The vicuña population fell from about 400,000 in the 1950s to roughly 10,000 by 1967.

Were it not for Felipe Benavides Barreda, an elegant former Peruvian diplomat and a graduate of the London School of Economics, the vicuña might have disappeared forever.

"I began to bellow and shout that there were no vicuña left," Benavides said in a New Yorker profile. "They said I was mad."

Benavides fought for reserves for the animals. In 1969, he helped establish the Pampas Galeras, a sixteen-thousand-acre vicuña sanctuary in Peru's southern altiplano that employed armed guards to protect the animals from poachers. He also authored the La Paz agreement between Peru and neighboring countries with vicuña populations, calling for a ten-year ban on hunting and trafficking in vicuña wool. European zoos protested the treaty, saying they needed to import vicuñas for their collections, but the agreement stuck. The penalty was one year in prison for every vicuña killed. Traders were given three to five years, with no possibility for bail. The authorities were finally getting serious. In 1975, vicuñas were listed on Appendix 1 (most endangered) of the Convention on International Trade in Endangered Species of Wild Flora and Fauna (CITES).

Though poachers were still operating and the Shining Path terrorist group hindered conservation activities into the 1990s, the population began to rebound. As the herds grew, the focus shifted from hands-off preservation to a policy of sustainable use. The vicuña, after all, had gold on its back and lived in a place where most of the indigenous people scraped along on about $300 a year. In 1995, the trade ban on cloth made from Peruvian fiber was lifted, and President Fujimori signed a law giving usufruct rights to the campesinos on whose communal land the animals lived. A consortium of three firms—the Italian companies Loro Piana and Agnona and the Peruvian company Inca Group—was awarded the rights to export and process the fiber.

The government also reinstated the *chaccu*, the ancient Inca model of sustainability. The plan called for rural Andeans to round up the vicuñas and shear and release them. The revenues from selling the raw fiber—roughly $100 for every animal shorn—would go to their communities. In exchange, they would protect the animals from poachers and do what they could to keep the population growing. By 1994, Peru had about 67,000 vicuñas; by 2010, there were close to 180,000. The International Union for Conservation of Nature (IUCN) reclassified the animal as "Least Concern."

The vicuña's odyssey back from the edge of extinction was one of the first demonstrations that conservation through sustainable use actually worked. Before the sustainability concept began to gain traction, the prevailing wisdom among animal-protection groups was that in order to save a species, you essentially had to put it under glass—and leave it alone to reproduce.

Though the population rebound is impressive, biologists, including Jane Wheeler, say the vicuña is still at risk. Poachers continue to kill animals for their fleece. In one particularly gruesome episode, in 2010, some 150 vicuñas, many of them newborns, were trapped and slaughtered in a remote area of southern Peru's highlands. The high market value of vicuña fleece has opened the door for unscrupulous middlemen and corruption. Climate change, meanwhile, threatens the animals' habitat, as does over-grazing on grasslands by domestic livestock.

At the same time, the government hatched captive manage-ment schemes that would keep the wild vicuña from roaming. Some communities have erected fences around their communal land, in an understandable but, Jane says, misguided attempt to keep their income-producers home. In many cases, the barriers were erected at the urging of a middleman, who stood to profit from an increase in fleece production. Jane believes the fences are stressful for the animals and could lead to inbreeding. She has made presentations in many rural communities to explain the hazards of keeping the vicuña enclosed.

"When we tell them about the bad things that can happen with corrals, they change their minds quickly," she says.

In her office, Jane looks at her computer screen and lets out a heavy sigh. She types, then pauses and stares at her computer monitor, and sighs again. She makes faces at the screen, then riffs through a few more minutes of emphatic tapping on the key-board. Then there is more sighing.

"I'm an academic," she says, finally, looking at me. "I don't know how I became the wicked witch."

After a few moments of silence, she narrows her eyes and fur-rows her brow, then moves her lips as if to say, "What?" She drops her shoulders, groans, and sits back in her chair.

Over the next several days, I will learn that Jane Wheeler's demeanor rides chiefly in the narrow lane between incredulity and exasperation. It is probably a universal trait among academics in obscure fields, who have spent much of their lives in the Sisyphean toil of untangling red tape and grubbing for grants. And this is already turning into a particularly annoying day.

Peru LNG, the liquid-gas supplier, with investment money from Texas's Hunt Oil Company, has just completed a $3.8-billion liquefied-natural-gas plant and pipeline, which runs from the jungle, over the Andes, to the Pacific. Since the pipes slice through wildlife habitat and mountain villages, the corporation was obligated to fund certain environmental and social-responsibility projects.

Jane's group is heading one such effort—a project that will teach improved vicuña fiber-shearing-and-processing techniques in three rural communities. She is just days away from taking her team—and me—to Huaytara, a small village in the mountains that is going to stage a *chaccu*. The $47,000 in funding from Peru LNG has been deposited into her account, but her bank won't give her access until she produces a sheaf of notarized documents demonstrating that the windfall is legitimate—and not, say, tied in to Peru's $20-billion cocaine trade. In the meantime, she's spending $500 a day of her own money to keep the project afloat.

"Raul," she calls wearily to her husband. "We have to go to the notary again."

It seems a simple enough task, but it will be hours before they return. There are plenty of notary publics in Lima, Jane tells me later. But finding one that is actually open for business, even during normal working hours—that's the challenge.

Jane and Raul live in a gated neighborhood above Pachacamac, a scrubby agricultural community south of Lima. When Jane drives toward the gatehouse, a guard comes out and lifts the spindly pole and waves her through. The security measures are reminders that this area was a hotbed of Sendero Luminoso—Shining Path—terrorist activity not too long ago. In 1992, the town's deputy mayor, Maria Elena Moyano, was murdered at a community barbecue.

The terrorists have retreated to the jungle, and these days the friction on Jane and Raul's street is apt to be over whose turn it is to get the irrigation water that is piped into the cement culverts that border the small fenced yards. Water from the Lurín River sustains a small garden behind Jane's one-story L-shaped adobe house. We walk out to the back yard and she shows me rows of manioc, lettuce, and squash. One spindly raspberry bush is propped up on a stake. In the front yard, hutches hold six guinea pigs and four rabbits—refugees from Raul's vaccination experiments. Gray doves, which sing monotonous, pan-fluty notes from dawn to dark, flit in the bushes.

Wheeler and Rosadio live in a world where ancient things are as common as gravel. Just down the road from their place—past the *chicharonnerias* selling fried pork rind and the farm stands and the empty lot where a dusty white llama sleeps among the rubble and the weeds—are the Pachacamac ruins, hundreds of acres of half-excavated ceremonial grounds and temples that date back to A.D. 200.

We drive by the ruins on our way to the office to pick up some CONOPA crew members for the trip into the mountains. "That's Pachacamac," Jane says, as if she were showing me where a new Wong's supermarket was going to be. From the road, it looks like a pockmarked sand hill surrounded by an abandoned construction site. "It's as significant as Machu Picchu."

By midafternoon, we and the CONOPA guys are speeding south, the chaos of Lima behind us. Under low clouds, the highway is a dark ribbon riding the contours of the desert coast: to our left, dunes corrugated by wind; to our right, the gray Pacific, creased by swells. I am in the backseat of the truck, one gear bag on my lap, another at my feet. Jane, holding a bag of groceries, is wedged between Andres, a long-legged Spanish vet student, and me. Two young men who are part of the field staff are up front: Alvaro, bearded and intense, is driving, and Antony, boyish and smiley, is riding shotgun. Only Jane and I speak English, but she has been conversing in Spanish for most of the trip so far. I have tried to catch scraps of recognizable words, but I've given up. They talk too fast and I have a headache.

Out my window, a cluster of decrepit shanties flashes by, then the quick colors of a lone fruit stand, the haunches of a scrounging dog, a bus barreling north, then more sand. I have read that this is one of the most arid places in the world, so dry that corpses dehydrate and mummify before they can decompose.

The monotony of the drive is interrupted by the frequent freight-train rumbling of big-rig trucks, whose drivers seem to keep themselves awake with adrenaline shots fueled by the thrill of passing us on the blindest of curves. This, I will learn as we make our way into the mountains, is a signature Peruvian move.

"Oh, *mi Dios*," I say, covering my eyes in the middle of one particularly risky-looking maneuver.

"*Sí, sí, mi Dios*," Alvaro repeats, laughing. "*Mi Dios*." The others smile and nod. I am happy to have amused the crew, but what I'm really thinking is, Please do not let me die on a highway in Peru.

More sand, more ocean, more crazy truck drivers, more sand—and then the surprise of green. We have reached the outskirts of Chincha, a coastal town that has the one thing that changes life in an arid land—a ribbon of river water. From where it began as snowmelt in the Andes, this water has been diverted hundreds, maybe thousands, of times into ancient irrigation ditches, feeding the roots of potatoes and maize on high terraces and alpine valleys, then, here at the coast, giving life to acres of cotton.

The traffic slows as the highway becomes Chincha's main street. We have joined a slow stream of brightly painted motorized rickshaws. Schoolchildren in uniforms walk in groups past women selling bales of raw white cotton from open-air shops. Beyond the outskirts of Chincha, the sun finally burns through the clouds in an angel-song display of crepuscular rays. The shafts pool light on the sea and illuminate a rocky islet spattered white with bird droppings.

This is, I remember reading, the Guano Coast, where the combination of millions of seabirds and a rainless climate guarantees that every surface large enough for bird feet will be permanently painted with dung. Early civilizations experimented with bird excrement as fertilizer and found that it coaxed astonishing bounty from the bad soil. Incan societies so prized the guano that the killing of seabirds during breeding season was declared a crime punishable by death. When, in the mid-1800s, European and American farmers discovered what Peruvian bird shit did for their crops, guano mining became a huge business. At the height of the forty-year guano boom, American and British ships crowded the rolling seas off the rock islands waiting—sometimes as long as three months—for their cargo holds to be filled with dung. The Industrial Revolution, the invention of man-made fertilizers, and the fact that the miners were starting to hit rock put an end to the guano rush.

We continue south through Pisco, a town of about sixty thousand that is famous for the production of the clear grape brandy that bears its name and is the key ingredient in the pisco sour, a potent cocktail made with lime juice and angostura bitters and topped with frothed egg white and fresh nutmeg. All along the road, locals have set up stands selling bottles of the liquor and advertising vineyard tours. The town was also briefly famous for being the epicenter of an 8.0-magnitude earthquake, which in 2007 shook Pisco for 210 terrifying seconds and nearly flattened it. Five hundred ninety-six people died. Three years later, the streets are still edged with rubble and the town is full of half-collapsed buildings.

Just past Pisco, we head inland on Los Libertadores, an ancient two-lane highway. The road skirts miles of lowland vineyards, then ascends through yellow foothills, and eventually crests on the broad tablelands of the high Andes. After a few hours of climbing, we turn off the highway in the dark and drive under a lighted stone gate that says BIENVENIDOS A HUAYTARA. The simple stone hotel we check into has a large, brightly lit lobby furnished with blocky laminate tables and modular sofas, giving it the feel, oddly, of a seventies ski-lodge rumpus room. Behind the front desk, three clerks sit close together watching a game show on a tiny TV.

Along with other members of the CONOPA staff who have arrived before us, we walk down Huaytara's main street, cross a small park, and head for the restaurant where Andres had called ahead for reservations—a table for nine. The place is dark. Andres knocks, and in a few moments the door opens a crack and a man peers out and says something to him.

"He says some other people came and he fed them and now he has run out of food," Jane reports, interpreting the conversation for me.

Next door is another café with a table big enough for our

group—and, it seems, plenty of food. I sense that there is a reason Andres wanted to go to the other restaurant, but it is eight-thirty and we are all hungry and cold. The guys order one bottle of Cristal beer and pass it with a small glass around the table. It's a charming Peruvian tradition of sharing that goes against my twin American urges to both guzzle my own beer and remain germ-free. Jane, sensing this, asks if I'd like my own glass. She gets one for herself, too, and orders another beer.

The menu says they have *cuy*—guinea pig—pork chops ("I can't recommend them," Jane leans over to say) and trout. I'm not opposed to guinea pig—I tried fried nuggets of it back in Lima and it wasn't bad—but when the plates are brought out, I'm glad I went with the trout. The *cuy* is large, breaded, fried, and disturbingly shaped like a flattened guinea pig.

Heading back, Jane and I duck into a little dirt-floor shop, where a small pyramid of tangerines glows in the dim light. We each buy a Coke so that we'll be able to have caffeine in the morning. Then, joining the others, we walk single file along the edge of the narrow street that leads to the hotel. A scrawny dog falls in behind us, trots along for a while, then gives up. The moon is nearly full, and from the hotel's stone patio I can see the deep grooves that funnel down the mountain flanks surrounding the town. And up there, beyond the indigo ridgeline, I picture the plateau and the mythic herds, awash in silver light.

At dawn, with the roosters starting up, I get a look at where we are. It's hard not to think Shangri-la thoughts as the sun breaks across the valley walls, illuminating the hilltop church that was once an Incan temple. By 6 A.M. we are in the cold truck, Antony and Alvaro up front and Jane and I in the back, washing down bananas and sweet crackers with Coke. Andres has gone ahead in the other CONOPA vehicle. For an hour we bump over the potholed pavement, gaining elevation with every switchback turn, until we reach the plateau and turn onto the dirt road that traverses it. The land here has the mottled look of desert camouflage; clay-beige sand tufted with pale fescue and bunch-grass, boulders flocked with gray-green lichen—and, beyond the rocky lunar flats, coppery hills and folds of dark canyons.

Jane points out the track of the buried liquid-natural-gas pipeline, a bare seam stitched across the steppe. Whatever else people think of the project, which turned Peru from an importer of gas to an exporter, no one disputes the fact that its construction was heroic. It took four years to run the line the 254 miles from the eastern flank of the Andes to the new liquefaction plant south of Lima. Before dropping west for the coast, it climbed to 16,080 feet. Engineers had to use a barometric chamber to find welding materials that would hold up in the thin air, and a *Guinness World Records* representative made the trek to the project's frozen apex to certify that it was, indeed, the highest pipeline in the world. Besides the altitude and the cold, there were the other standard Peruvian obstacles: wind, snow, earthquakes, landslides, tsunamis, flood, and drought, to say nothing of the political shenanigans and violent protests that dogged the project right up until the day the spigot was turned and the first gas flowed to the liquefaction plant.

And it is the gas, of course, that has brought Jane and her team to the altiplano. She is spending Hunt Oil pipeline money—or will be spending it, as soon as the bank releases it to her. Funding from the deep pockets of the Peru LNG project should keep her research going for years, she has told me.

The dirt scar disappears into the distance.

And then I see them. On a ridge, three long-necked animals stand in silhouette against the morning sky, backlit and lovely.

"Oh," I say, "I think . . ."

"Vah-koon-ya," Jane says quietly, sounding like a proud parent. I pull my camera out of its case, and Jane speaks in Spanish to Alvaro. He stops the truck and I roll down the window and lean out into the frigid air to take pictures.

"*Bonita*," I say when we get under way again. "*Mucho bonita*." I know that isn't quite right, but Antony and Alvaro smile and nod.

"*Mira*." Antony points ahead and I see more vicuñas—one small herd on a bare hill, their ivory chests bright in the sun, and then another group, grazing close to the road. We go by and they raise their heads and stare, taking us in—a black truck, rolling slowly, kicking up dust.

After about thirty minutes, we reach the *chaccu* site. It is a wide place in the road, bordered by two low stone buildings. An outhouse stands alone in a rocky expanse, its wooden door half off its hinges. The other CONOPA truck is already here. Parked near it is a shiny white bus with curtained green-tinted windows and futuristic-looking sculpted side mirrors. The words COMUNIDAD CAMPESINA DE HUAYTARA are painted on the side.

"That's the community bus," Jane says, as we unload our gear. "They bought it with vicuña money."

It's the first evidence I've seen that the vicuña management program is yielding dividends for the campesinos. That they purchased this fancy coach, in all its incongruous touring-rock-star glory, seems funny and a little sad, like a late-model Escalade in front of a dilapidated trailer. But it is a good-looking bus and it must make the townspeople proud.

We cross the road and head to the top of a rise where there is a makeshift corral, about twenty yards across and seven feet high and surrounded by burlap. From it, two lengths of net-lined fencing splay out down the hill in an ever-widening V. Antony sets up a video camera near the fence and points the lens down the slope. Jane and the CONOPA crew converse in Spanish. I can tell by the way they slap their hands together and stamp their feet that they are talking about how cold it is.

I walk away from them and find a rock to sit on. I feel light-headed in the thin air, and my heart is racing. I will wait here, with my hands in my pockets, my chin tucked down behind the collar of my down jacket. The wind picks up and I pull my Red Sox cap down. For a moment, I see myself from above: alone on a rock, on the roof of the world, because of an overcoat hanging in a cedar-lined closet in a skyscraper in Vancouver, two pins on a map connected by a tenuous thread. It seems at once hilariously inconsequential and frighteningly profound. I look out over the burnt-yellow plain, scanning for signs of the roundup. But there is nothing to see yet, just the blue of the morning sky and the faint, tissue-paper disk of last night's moon.

For the next hour, the campesinos and the CONOPA crew work on erecting a large blue tent, a gift to the community from Peru LNG and a key component of Jane's project. It is designed to make the shearing process more efficient, and less vulnerable to the elements.

"The fleece used to just blow away," Jane tells me.

Inside, there are stations for clipping, cleaning, and weighing the fleece. There is also a triage corner for any animals that might need medical treatment. Though the *chaccu* is based on Incan tradition, no one alive has memories of it, so it is open to interpretation. Some communities, especially those that attract tourists, have been encouraged by private companies with stakes in the sale of the fiber to stage elaborate costumed pageants—and even to allow audience participation. Others, like this one way off the tourism grid, are all business. The participants are in jeans, windbreakers, and baseball caps.

The only nod to ritual was a small, private ceremony that was held the night before the roundup. On the mountaintop above Huaytara, Jane told me, the local shaman had lit on fire a container holding an alpaca fetus, cocoa leaves, and alpaca fat as an offering to the gods. A strong flame that completely consumed the contents of the tin would portend a successful *chaccu;* one that sputtered and died said the vicuña would not come.

I scan the horizon again and again, until finally, way off, I see movement. It is a kind of light-brown wave, cresting a distant knoll. Antony walks to his camera and looks through the viewfinder. The CONOPA guys are pointing down the hill. I head back over to Jane, who is now standing near the fence.

"Is that them?" I say. The wave is coming closer, and what seemed solid is now unraveling, streamers of tawny brown moving across the hill, then doubling back. As the herd gets closer, I can see that there are a hundred vicuñas, maybe more, running toward us. Behind them, a line of villagers holding a long rope festooned with colored streamers is pressing them forward. Adult and baby animals run along the fence line and traverse the rocky slope, looking for escape. Dust rises as they sprint up the hill toward the corral. Larger vicuñas try to leap the barrier and a few make it out. A small one gets caught up in the fencing and falls, its legs frantically bicycling in the air, until onlookers extricate it from the netting. Some stop in their tracks, nostrils flaring, then dip their heads and run again.

Children in hooded sweatshirts and dirt-caked sneakers join

the men for the last stage of the roundup, laughing and urging the vicuñas into the corral chute until, at last, every animal has squeezed into the enclosure and the gate has been closed behind them. I walk over and peer through an opening in the burlap panels. The animals stand still, eyes big, ears erect. They are remarkably calm. A few bleat softly. They smell damp and peaty.

When the shearing team is ready to start, they enter the corral, chase down an animal, pick it up in their arms, and carry it out. They stop first at the entrance to the tent for inspection by the CONOPA vets. If the vicuña is too young or has recently been shorn, it is released. If it has a kind of dandruff that makes the fiber undesirable, blood and skin scrapings are taken to be studied later, and then it is set free. If it is deemed healthy and has a full coat, it is fitted with a black hood. Though this is meant to keep the animal calm, the hood makes it look as if it's about to face a firing squad.

Inside the tent, the animal is splayed out on a low wooden platform, its front and hind legs restrained and held tight by helpers. It's hard to look at this without thinking of sacrificial altars. But this is a haircut, not a bloodletting. With electric clippers powered by a noisy generator, a skilled shearer removes the fleece from the back of the animal in one piece. The fluff is rolled, like a length of weightless sod, and delivered to the cleaning tables. Here two women with tissue plugs in their nose, so they won't inhale the fine fibers or dust, shake the fleece over a screen table, pick out bits of grass and coarse hair, then place it in clear plastic bags. Then it is weighed and recorded and added to the stockpile. Later, the fleece will be warehoused, and eventually sold to spinners and weavers, most likely in either the U.K. or Italy.

When the shearing is done, the vicuña is carried to the exit doorway of the tent and the black hood is yanked off. The animal stands frozen for a moment, blinking and sniffing the air—long enough for me to take pictures, which I do from behind a big rock—and then takes a few steps: a meandering uncertain trot, at first, then a more determined run down the hill to freedom.

It goes on all day, the wrangling and shearing. Though the work is hard, the mood is lighthearted. When an animal wriggles out of the arms of a handler, he and the crowd of onlookers laugh. Occasionally, a worker lets a child cradle a very young vicuña before it is released. The windowless tent warms as the morning goes by: more black hoods, more animals on the table, more humming clippers, more frantic hooves reaching for solid ground. The clear bags of tawny fluff mount up.

Late into the afternoon, the work continues. The campesinos have made the unusual decision to do a second roundup, and the corral is full again. We will be here for a while. I head over to the stone house and find Jane sitting on a bench. There is a big pot of something warming over a fire, attended to by a trio of local women in long embroidered skirts and flat-topped brimmed straw hats. One of them hands me a bowl of the clear broth, in which there are chunks of soft potato and a meaty knuckle of bone. "Alpaca, maybe?" Jane says, when I ask what she thinks it is. I stand by the fire and eat it—alpaca or not—grateful for the warmth of the bowl in my hands.

The temperature continues to drop as the sun dips toward the horizon and paints the altiplano in a pink honeyed light. Kids playing soccer on a dirt expanse near the house cast long shadows across the road. Jane and I get into the truck to try to get warm.

I ask her how many animals she thinks they will have shorn by the end of the day.

"Maybe two hundred. Worth about twenty-five thousand dollars.

"This was a good one," she says. "You were lucky. Sometimes they don't happen. An assistant of mine once walked for a few days to get to a really remote *chaccu* site, and when she got there they said they had done it the day before. She missed it. You never know."

We take turns playing solitaire on her laptop and run the car to get some heat. Then we sit in silence, listening to the generator whir. It is getting cold again.

"I was just thinking," Jane says after a while. "You know . . . I get so beaten down by the politics and everything. It's sort of surprising . . . that all of this happened because of me, because of the work we've done."

Finally, the shearing is finished and the trucks are loaded. We start the slow descent back to Huaytara. Antony flips through a CD case, selects one, and says something to Alvaro. Antony smiles and slides it into the slot on the dashboard. The music plays. It's a liquid, ripe Caribbean-sounding jazz, and for some reason, under the high white moon on the spine of the Andes, it sounds just right. I stare out the window as we roll slowly around hairpin curves, our headlights occasionally illuminating Spanish-language road signs with exclamation points that I interpret as warnings about fog and falling rocks and narrow bridges and impending *muerte*.

Tomorrow, the vicuñas, shaved down to nappy plush, will be back on the steppe. The bags of fleece will be locked in a store-house. The campesinos will return to the *chaccu* site to disassemble the blue tent and pack it away until next time. We'll head to Lima. Jane will go back to her battles with the bank, and I'll spend some time in the city on my own. I will have my first pisco sour, and my second. And in a high-end clothing store in Lima's Larcomar, an open-air shopping complex above the fogged-over

Pacific, I'll watch a tourist pick up a vicuña scarf and rub it between her fingers and thumb. Then she'll put it down and walk away and think nothing more about that soft, pretty thing, too expensive to buy.

As we make the last turn and drive under Huaytara's gate, I reach down and feel around my feet and realize that I left my empty camera bag by the rock where I had been sitting. I liked that bag. I bought it at Best Buy for $35, just for this trip. I picture it up there in the dark, lid unzipped, open to the big sky. And then I decide. I won't think of it as a loss. I will think of it as an offering.

CHAPTER 3

The Lining

John Cutler spent the next several days thinking about the overcoat. An idea began to take shape. He was fifty-five years old. He had no successors. He was well aware that he was the last Cutler who would ever wield the family shears. His two grown sons had no interest in taking over—and why would they? Bespoke tailoring was a dying art. Cheap offshore manufacturing and an obsession with designer labels had brought custom-made to its knees—and a lack of young people willing to put in the years required to learn the trade would finish it off.

What if he called on everything he knew about his craft to make this coat? What if he and his trusted workroom team made it entirely by hand—without a single machine stitch? What if he used the finest materials he could get his hands on? He already had the vicuña, of course, but what if he achieved that level of perfection with all the other components? Everything he used to make the coat would come from craftsmen who were as obsessed with quality as he was.

When Keith came in to be measured, John opened a bottle of wine—a buttery New South Wales Chardonnay—and told him what he was envisioning.

"I trust you," Keith had said. "Do whatever you like."

Then he had handed the tailor his black American Express card and said, "Take what you need." He had not asked then—and he would never ask—how much the coat would cost.

John got to work gathering the materials that he would need.

Some were easy. He already had premium silk threads and top-of-the-line horsehair canvases, which would be required to give the garment its shape.

The lining, however, was trickier. The fabrics he had on the premises wouldn't do. They were viscose blends—hardwearing and practical, yes, but this coat was not about practicality. It was about luxury. There was no question that the lining must be silk—and not just any silk. Only a few companies in the world produced the kind of quality John wanted. Hermès was one. He considered the possibility of stitching together several of the superb scarves. Stefano Ricci was another. John sold Stefano's ties in the shop. Perhaps he could take some apart and fashion them into a patchwork lining. Then he got to wondering—why not just ask Stefano if would sell him a length of his silk?

John had done business with the enigmatic Florentine menswear designer for years. He knew the designer's agent in Melbourne, so he gave him a call to ask if he thought Stefano might be willing to sell him some silk. Out of the question, the agent had said. Mr. Ricci would never do that—certainly not to be used as a lining. John sensed that the agent was reluctant to even approach the designer, but he kept pressing.

Tell him it is for a vicuña overcoat, entirely handmade, John said, believing Stefano Ricci would appreciate that kind of commitment to artisanship. Tell him it will be of the highest standard. Mention that the coat is navy blue—he would defer to Mr. Ricci's good taste as to the specifics of the lining design as long as it complemented the fabric's hue. Two months went by, and John heard nothing. And then, one day, he got a call. It was the agent. He sounded dumbfounded. Stefano Ricci would sell him enough silk to line one overcoat. But, the designer had insisted, he must tell no one—and he must never ask again.

We are all Adam's children, but silk makes the difference.

ENGLISH PROVERB

I am sitting in a dark-orange club chair, made from the skin of wild New Guinean crocodiles, waiting for Stefano Ricci to arrive. This is something I may never do again, so I am paying particular attention to the soft window-paned leather and to the perplexing, almost unnameable hue—persimmon, is it, or just a half shade more toward paprika? The chair, and others like it, are placed in pairs on a travertine tiled floor in Stefano Ricci's eponymous boutique, set theatrically in the former armory of the Palazzo Tornabuoni, on one of Florence's choicest shopping streets. Art-filled upper floors of the fifteenth-century palace, once the home of a Renaissance-era pope, have recently been converted into a private-residence club managed by the Four Seasons. (Owners are picked up at the airport in the club's Maserati.) With upstairs neighbors like that, and a retail block that includes Bulgari, Gucci, Louis Vuitton, and Cartier, it is obvious why Stefano Ricci opened his flagship store here in 2009. The location is ideal for snaring the kinds of customers—think petroleum-rich princelings—who crave the sixty-one-year-old designer's exquisite handmade menswear.

From my seat, I can see the Stefano Ricci spring 2011 collection, displayed with spare and artful precision on burled-walnut tables and in tall wardrobes. There are lavender-and-lime striped Egyptian-cotton dress shirts, dimpled ostrich bomber jackets, tissue-weight wool suits, slender pointy shoes, and trays of tonally grouped whorled silk ties—all set off by silver elephant-tusk sculptures and large vases filled with exuberant, waxy-looking tropical blooms. A well-groomed salesman stands with his hands clasped behind his back, and a security guard hovers near the door. Both have smiled at me, but I get the distinct feeling they harbor a certain dubiousness about my presence. There are no customers in the store on this unusually warm morning in late March. I shift my position in the squared-off chair and jiggle my foot. Outside, a church bell rings and groups of tourists walk by heading toward the Duomo, a few blocks away.

And then Stefano Ricci arrives. His entrance into the store is operatic—an audible sweeping in. He is short and wide, with a spectacular mane of longish salt-and-pepper hair swept back and curling past his collar, a full white beard, and dark, playful eyes behind rimless glasses. His suit is a wonder of fluid navy wool, cut just so to broaden the shoulders and skim the ample torso: a bear in a man-suit.

"Mrs. Noo-nan," he says in a little song that trails off into a sigh. I rise to shake his hand and the hand of Filippo Ricci, Stefano's trim twenty-seven-year-old son and the company's R&D manager, who is at his side, looking efficient and thoroughly exfoliated. I sit back down. Stefano takes a chair behind a desk, and Filippo takes the chair next to mine, pulls an iPad from a black leather case, and puts it on his lap.

"You don't mind if I smoke," Stefano says, pulling a cigarette from a pack. He points one finger skyward toward the stained-glass panels forty feet overhead. "High ceilings." An elegant blond woman places coffee in a very small porcelain cup on Stefano's desk, adjacent to his right hand. He looks at me and takes a long draw on his cigarette.

"So," he says. It took months of emails to get this meeting arranged. I'm still not sure what he is willing to do. I'm hoping for at least twenty pure minutes of Stefano Ricci time. I clear my throat and ask him how he got started in the menswear business.

As a boy in Florence, Stefano was an enthusiastic doodler, filling the margins of his school papers with small figures, paisleys, and swirls. He also had an unusual obsession with neckties—Hermès neckties, to be specific—and by the age of twenty he had amassed 150 of them. His mother, who was in the clothing business, connected the odd dots and suggested that young Stefano put some of his drawings on his own neckwear. He started making silk ties and found that he couldn't stop.

"It was like a fever," he tells me.

Even after forty years, every design starts with Stefano noodling around on paper with a fountain pen—often late at night, in a miasma of smoke, with opera music blaring. His ties are made entirely by hand, using only the best raw silk and the most labor-intensive printing process. The finished products are vivid wonders that beg to be fondled: luminous, soft, and supple, but substantial enough to produce a beefy Windsor knot and a deep, authoritative dimple. The designer's neckties, which start at $200 for a basic model and go as high as $35,000 for a limited-edition one studded with diamonds, are considered by many tie aficionados to be the best in the world.

"My passion . . . is to design ties, for the opportunity to play with color and with warp and weft," Stefano says. "I am not an artist. I am not talented. I am a technician of cloth. And I must say that I do everything from start to finish. It is one of the privileges of the profession."

From neckties, Stefano moved on to shirts of the finest Egyptian cotton—always with his signature octagonal mother-of-pearl buttons and contrast microstitching on the collar and cuffs. He branched out to crocodile belts and platinum cufflinks and silk robes. Every item is made one at a time by a team of two hundred artisans, either in the designer's small factory just outside Florence or in nearby ateliers.

Like other Florentine fashion designers who preceded him— Salvatore Ferragamo, Guccio Gucci, Emilio Pucci, Roberto Cavalli—Stefano Ricci grew up in a world where the virtuosity of the artistic hand was a daily fact: not just in the city center's architecture, paintings, and sculptures but in tiny workshops across the green waters of the Arno River. There, in the Oltrarno, shoemakers, carvers, tailors, weavers, and goldsmiths were carrying on the legacies of the medieval craft guilds, formed, in part, to assure the quality of the work. Their predecessors' skills had helped make Florence the epicenter of fashion and style during the Renaissance, a position the city held until the seventeenth century, when Paris began to overshadow it in all things cultural.

In 1951, Giovanni Battista Giorgini, a savvy local straw-hat exporter who was determined to get Florence back on the sartorial map, staged a small fashion show in his villa and invited American apparel buyers. Eight buyers and one journalist for *Women's Wear Daily* stopped in on their way home from seeing the Paris collections. *WWD* ran a front-page article about the show and the emergence of Italian style.

The ripple of interest generated there had turned into a tidal wave by the time Giorgini presented a larger show in July 1952, this time in the Sala Bianca of the Palazzo Pitti. Buyers were dazzled by the refined but relaxed clothing—and by the scenery, the food, and the parties. It didn't hurt that the clothes were about half the price of French fashions, or that several of the featured designers and couturiers, including Contessa Simonetta Visconti, Princess Giovanna Caracciolo, and Marchese Emilio Pucci, were bona-fide aristocrats—even if, as the fashion historian Nicola White points out, some were in financial straits following the war. On a hot July evening, under the crystal-and-gold chandeliers in the white ballroom of a palace that had been home to grand dukes and kings, the Americans fell hard for the romance of Giorgini's ahead-of-its-time marketing message: that craftsmanship mattered, that heritage mattered, that provenance mattered. "Made in Italy" was on its way to becoming what it would remain for the next sixty years—a label that instantly conferred quality, sophistication, and connoisseurship—and stamped your visa for entry into *la dolce vita.*

In 1955, the Pitti show attracted five hundred buyers and two hundred journalists. A menswear-only version of the show debuted in 1972; Stefano Ricci was there with his first homegrown neckwear collection. Neiman Marcus ordered his ties, as did Bergdorf Goodman and Harrods and Holt Renfrew. Over the next thirty-five-plus years, Stefano showed time and again that, besides being a talented designer, he had sharp marketing instincts and a nose for new money. He was one of the first European luxury brands to open in China, starting with Shanghai in 1993, then adding stores in Beijing, Chengdu, Hangzhou, Macau, and Xi'an.

"Everybody thought I was crazy [to go to China]," he says.

By the summer of 2011, Stefano had boutiques all over the world—some owned, some licensed. Uniform in their décor—always the croc, the dark wood, and the tile—the stores are designed to feel like international branches of an exclusive men's club. His jet-setting customers seek the stores. Stefano could map out their travels by looking at where they placed their special orders.

"We already had a store in Beverly Hills, but we are opening a new one, much bigger, in the fall," Stefano says. "Filippo, show madam."

Filippo taps the screen of his iPad and turns it toward me.

"It's the most famous spot in Beverly Hills," he says. I recognize the wedged-shaped store, at 2 Rodeo Drive, that had been the Gianfranco Ferré boutique.

Stefano doesn't like to say who his customers are, but it has been reported that Hosni Mubarak, Nelson Mandela, Tom Cruise, Robert De Niro, Mikhail Gorbachev, the Sultan of Brunei, and Prince Moosa of Bangladesh all wear Stefano Ricci. Most Ricci devotees are not celebrities, however; they are anonymous, worldly rich men who have developed a craving for the particularly potent sartorial crack that Stefano Ricci pushes.

"I design my clothes for people who don't need my clothes," Stefano says. "They are attracted by the idea of having something special. They try once, and they want more, because they feel good in what they are wearing. Thanks to God, they get addicted—they want to possess."

The Stefano Ricci empire grew even as the recession deepened and the costs of silk, cotton, wool, and leather soared. Second-tier brands scrambled to cut costs by skimping on details and hoping no one would notice. Stefano went the other way, designing his products to be even more labor-intensive, more extravagant in their materials, more niche.

"Even if my loyal clients go through a crisis, they don't avoid doing things for their own pleasure," he tells me. "They still want to feel that energy, that power. You still want to look good. And, honestly, if you have a billion dollars and you lose half a billion, your lifestyle doesn't change."

By 2010, worldwide sales of luxury goods were surging again, fueled by double-digit growth in China and signs of recovery in the United States and in some European markets. The number of millionaires in Asia surpassed Europe in 2011 and was expected to surpass those in North America in the near future. By 2012, Chinese consumers would account for more than 20 percent of global luxury sales. Much to Stefano Ricci's delight, Chinese men were the ones driving the spending spree, shelling out $1.1 billion annually for high-end apparel. And their tastes were changing; once obsessed only with buying instantly identifiable status labels, they were starting to develop a deeper understanding of and appreciation for the craftsmanship and heritage behind a product.

"My business in Asia is unbelievable," Stefano says, chopping at the air for emphasis.

Still, there are places the Stefano Ricci brand doesn't play well.

"Florentines come and have a look around and they say, 'Stefano, your shop is for new money.' And I say, 'Yes, because old money doesn't spend!' People say Florentines 'have short arms.' There are a lot of aristocrats here, but they don't shop."

Stefano laughs and lights another cigarette.

I ask him about the silk lining for Keith Lambert's coat.

"Yes, I remember John Cutler asking me for fabric. I don't ever do that, give my linings to someone else. But he's a sweet person, Mr. Cutler, a good man, a real clothing man. There are not so many left. . . . You know," he goes on, "I would be very pleased to have you see where my ties and linings are printed in Como. If you would be able to have the time."

"I'd like that," I say.

"You can see where we made the lining for the coat. It is the last factory in Como where things are printed only by hand."

Filippo and Stefano have a conversation in Italian that I can't understand. They get on their cell phones, hang up, have another animated discussion, and then make more calls.

"So, it is confirmed," Stefano says when he finally puts the phone down. "You take the train tonight. You will be my guest."

Just then, Stefano's eyes light up when he sees a stocky older woman come through the doors.

"Ah," he says, standing to greet her warmly.

"Signor Ricci," she says, and they converse in Italian. When she leaves, he tells me that she is one of his seamstresses, recently retired. "She was walking by the store and she saw me in here— I'm never here! And she was so happy to see me, she wanted to stop and say hello. She was with me for twenty-two years— wonderful woman."

Stefano's cell phone rings again. While he talks, I look at my small notebook. There are so many questions I have yet to ask. I want to know, for one thing, how he defines "luxury." Stefano puts down the phone. His eyes narrow as he draws in smoke.

"I think you are a writer—not, thanks to God, a journalist," he says, leaning back in his chair. "You can't believe the things I get asked over and over. 'What is luxury, Mr. Ricci? How do you define "luxury," Mr. Ricci?'"

I put my notebook in my lap.

"The word 'luxury' has been diluted," Stefano says, and I realize that he is going to answer the question anyway. "I went to a conference on luxury in Moscow five or six years ago. I was giving a talk. I told the audience, 'I am very sorry to tell you that there is no more luxury. Luxury is dead.' Everyone was shocked. I told them that companies that don't have any idea about luxury have abused the word. I said we need a new word. I suggested 'excellence.' It is a good word, but now everyone uses 'excellence.' "

Stefano goes on, unprodded.

"I wrote a book called *Luxor of Egypt* with my friend Zahi Hawass, the minister of state for antiquities—you know, the Egyptian tomb hunter; he's always in *National Geographic*, in the hat? And in it I said, 'Luxury is a fresh glass of water in the desert, luxury is friendship, luxury is love, luxury is health. When you are exhausted, to reach the peak of a mountain, that is luxury.' "

Luxury, it must also be said, is the very sweet convertible Jaguar in which I later find myself riding shotgun, tearing through the streets of Florence, with Filippo at the wheel. We are following his father to Fiesole and the green hills just outside the city, where the Riccis live and have their factory. Stefano Ricci has invited me to lunch.

Cypress trees line the long driveway that climbs a lazy S-curve toward Il Salviatino, a honey-colored fifteenth-century villa that was once the summer hunting lodge of a cardinal and has just been opened as a five-star hotel. Three men join us— a banker from Milan and two Stefano Ricci managers, whose close-shaved chins are only just starting to shadow. All are in slim dark suits, and all have on bright silk neckties.

We are shown to the outside terrace and seated at a round table under a white canopy. There are clipped geometric gardens below the terrace and, beyond them, under the milky sky, a view of all Florence. Waiters stand at the ready just beyond white leather chesterfield sofas, hustling over whenever Stefano Ricci seems close to making a request. "Now, what to drink?" Stefano says to me. "Champagne, I think. And to eat? What do you like?"

"Oh, I don't know. Everything," I say.

"So, allow me. I take responsibility."

Conversations in Italian effervesce around me. I sip my champagne and look out at the distant bald knob of the Duomo, bobbing above a choppy red-roof sea. A plate of pillowy *ricotta gnudi*, garnished with gray-green leaves of sage, is placed in front of me.

"When this hotel opened," Stefano says, "we were very happy."

"We come here a lot," Filippo says, and I get it. To them, this is the corner deli—a place to grab lunch.

Stefano tells me that he is about to open a new factory just over the hill from where we are sitting.

"It is big enough to hold all my toys," he says, laughing.

Among them, he says, are a collection of hunting trophies bagged on Ricci family safaris, including an upright, full-grown polar bear, a North American mountain goat, dozens of wild boars, and tusks from an African elephant. Each summer Stefano and his wife, Claudia, along with Filippo and Niccolò, Stefano's thirty-year-old son, who is the company's CEO, pack suitcases full of custom-made khakis, leather boots, pith helmets, and hunting rifles ("You have no idea how hard it is to get permission to bring them on an airplane," Filippo tells me later) and head off in pursuit of big game. Their expeditions have taken them from the Yukon to Pakistan to Bolivia.

"As a boy, I was always running away from school during hunting season," Stefano says. "It was like a religion. My great-uncle would say, 'Let's go,' and we'd take off into the hills. I would come back to school with pheasants and boar. Then the priests don't mind so much that I was gone."

The Riccis spend three weeks every summer in Tanzania.

"I hunt for a few hours, and then I spend the rest of the day designing my next collection. People think I'm crazy, working on my holiday, but it's not working. For me, it is a joy. I'm able to focus, to have a clear view, away from the world of tailoring and fashion," he says. "I always select a camp near a big river, in the middle of nowhere. We have a satellite phone—only for emergencies. It is a joy to be able to share my passion with my family, to be out there with all the persons I care about.

"This year, I am going after a prehistoric monster in Rukwa. A giant crocodile. Huge," he says, and I have to suppress the urge to laugh out loud. "Filippo has the record, with five and a half meters, and I am going for six meters. You have to be silent when you hunt crocodile. You can't let a twig snap. And you have to shoot them in the temple from a hundred and fifty meters. If you miss by just a little, you lose him."

A waiter puts a plate of braised beef cheeks in an eggy sauce in front of me, and another refills my champagne glass, then Stefano's. I ask Stefano what other toys he has.

"I collect vintage cars," he replies, but won't say how many when I ask. "I have . . . quite a few. They are mostly Aston Martins from the fifties. Every year, my wife and sons, we all drive in the Mille Miglia."

I have read about this race; it's a thousand-mile vintage-sports-car road rally from Brescia to Rome and back. Stefano is one of the sponsors.

"I'm driving this year with Burt Tansky—you know, from Neiman Marcus. It's fantastic—millions of Italians line the streets. And we present the Stefano Ricci Gentleman Driver trophy to the team whose outfits best match their car. I sleep for three days when it is over."

I ask him if he practices for the race.

"This Saturday I am taking my car for a test drive. We'll

drive it to the sea and back—a few hours. I am sorry to say you cannot come. It's too dangerous. Those old cars have very little brake system. In the race, once in a while someone dies."

A perfect cylinder of cream and mascarpone layered with chocolate wafers and topped with fresh raspberries is placed before me.

"Oh, I love that," Filippo says, eyeing my dessert.

Stefano calls for the chef. When he appears, Stefano pumps his hand and speaks to him in effusive Italian, obviously complimenting him on the meal. Then a hotel employee appears with a long envelope and hands it to me. It is a train ticket for the 5 P.M. trip to Como, via Milan.

"Now you go see my silk. Then you know why Stefano Ricci is so expensive," Stefano says with a sly smile.

According to Confucius, the story of silk begins in 2640 B.C., when a cocoon, most likely that of the native *Bombyx mandarina* moth, fell out of a mulberry tree into the teacup of a fourteen-year-old Chinese empress. When she fished it out of the hot liquid, the cocoon unraveled, revealing itself to be one long, shimmering filament. Her discovery led to an intensive study of the moth, and when its life cycle was understood the Chinese began to practice sericulture, the breeding of silkworms in captivity, in order to harvest raw silk. The story may be more myth than fact, but what is certain is that over the next thousand years of domestication the silk moth evolved into a species known as *Bombyx mori*; flightless, blind, and dependent on its captors, its only mission is to mate and lay hundreds of poppy-seed-size eggs.

The life of a silkworm is at once pedestrian and profound. When the eggs hatch, the tiny larvae embark on an almost non-stop eating binge, plowing their way through layer after layer of white mulberry leaves, their food of choice. In a breeding room, where hundreds of thousands of worms are feeding, it is said that the sound is like that of a steady rain on a tin roof. After thirty-two days, when the caterpillar has multiplied its weight by ten thousand and shed its skin four times, it begins to spin a cocoon by moving its head from side to side in a figure-eight pattern, extruding from two glands under its jaw a liquid that—in an amazing trick of chemistry—becomes solid as soon as it hits the air. The larva spins continuously for three days, shrinking as it constructs its white, multilayered oval pod.

Left alone, the moth would soon break out of the cocoon and the cycle would begin again. But when harvesting high-quality silk is the goal, the moth must be killed inside the cocoon before it damages the mile-long silk filament. This is usually done by boiling it to death. Animal-rights advocates have pushed for humane silk-harvesting practices. There is a small market for Ahimsa, or Peace, silk, made from the broken fibers of cocoons after the moth has been allowed to emerge naturally, but the silk is less lustrous and far more expensive than silk produced in the traditional way. Scientists have also been studying how to get at silk produced by wild caterpillars, whose cocoons have a hard coating that makes unraveling almost impossible. In 2011, researchers from England and Kenya discovered a way to remove that mineral layer without damaging the fibers using an acidic solution—something that could help open the door to a lucrative industry in poor countries where there is a large population of wild caterpillars.

Silkworms are extremely sensitive; expose them to cool temperatures, drafts, loud noises, humidity, tobacco smoke, even the smell of sweat or extra-sweet perfume, and they may produce inferior silk or no silk at all. Few creatures have been studied as extensively as the *Bombyx mori*. In the past several decades, research on silkworms and moths has led to major discoveries about genetics, heredity, the brain, and the mysteries of sexual attraction. Pheromones, for instance, were first isolated and identified when scientists realized that one sexually ready female silkworm moth could attract every male moth within a mile, just by giving off a minuscule amount of scent through the nanotunnels in her antennae.

More recently, researchers have blasted silkworms with an electric field to induce them to spin more durable silk, fed them dyed leaves to coax them to produce colored silk, and even implanted them with spider genes to get them to spin a hybrid version of Kevlar-strong spider dragline silk. (Since spiders are cannibalistic, raising them in groups for raw silk has so far proved to be an exercise in futility.) Researchers at Tufts University have applied their knowledge of caterpillars to design soft-bodied robots. Taiwanese engineers have used silk proteins in transistors to increase the page-turning speed of e-books.

For more than two thousand years, the Chinese guarded the secret of silk. Anyone who dared to smuggle eggs, worms, or moths over the border was executed. Eventually, the secret leaked out, first to Korea, then to Japan, Persia, India, and Arabia. Sericulture made it to the West in the middle of the sixth century, when two monks, sent by the Byzantine emperor Justinian, sneaked silkworm eggs and seeds from the mulberry tree across the border by hiding them in hollow bamboo walking staffs. Four hundred years later, King Roger of Sicily captured Greek silk weavers, brought them back to Palermo, and set them up in a silk-making operation in his palace. From Sicily, silkworm breeding moved to Northern Italy, where forests of white mulberry trees were planted in order to ensure a constant food supply for the voracious larvae. In a bid to boost an economy dragged down by the faltering wool trade, Italian rulers moved sericulture to the tranquil shores of Lago di Como, a long, deep divining-rod-shaped lake on the Swiss border, about twenty-five miles north of Milan.

The sky is dark when my train pulls into the Como station. Elisa Panzeri, a petite forty-year-old Demi Moore look-alike with straight espresso-colored hair and an even smile, has been sent by Stefano to meet me. Elisa is in the silk business, which should come as no surprise, because, until very recently, almost everyone in this small two-thousand-year-old city on the tip of the south-western fork of the lake had a hand in the silk trade.

We drive north a few miles on Via Regina, to Cernobbio, and find a place to park. Across the narrow lake, lights give contour to the ridgeline that snakes for thirty miles along the eastern shore. The town is quiet now, except for the easy slap of water against the dock and the insect whine of a motorbike climbing into the hills. Come summer, though, the plane-tree-lined prom-enade will be filled with tourists stupefied by the beauty of the place: the high alpine peaks to the north, the extravagant water-front palazzos with their terraced gardens, and the people—the people!—stepping ashore from the polished mahogany decks of Riva speedboats; women with cascading hair, stilettos, and tight dresses, and men in open shirts, flat-front trousers, and pastel loafers, looking as if they're headed for a long, Bellini-soaked lunch with George Clooney, perhaps, whose twin villas are just down the road.

Mr. Clooney, alas, is not in the Trattoria del Vapore tonight. At a table near a stone fireplace, Elisa and I work our way through beef tartare, *risotto con pesce*, and a bottle of white wine as she tells me about her family. Her father, a longtime friend of Stefano Ricci's, started his own silk-screening business in 1974. By then, disease and high costs had wiped out the silkworm population and sericulture was no longer being practiced in Italy, but the Comaschis, as Como residents are called, were doing amazing things with the raw silk they were importing from China. No one—not even the esteemed silk workers of Lyon, France—could match their skills in finishing, dyeing, and printing fabric. The designers knew it, and a parade of them came through Como to source their silks: among them Ferragamo, Pucci, Gucci, Oscar de la Renta, Yves Saint Laurent, Mary Quant, John Galliano, Ralph Lauren, and Gianni Versace. These days, Panzeri's biggest customer is Stefano Ricci.

"He spends a lot of time in Como," Elisa says. "He was here for ten days before the Pitti. He is always working. He's up early to talk to China and stays up late to talk to L.A. With Mr. Ricci, it is expected we go two hundred miles an hour."

This is more than a figure of speech, I discover. In a few months, Elisa will be driving in the Mille Miglia road rally with Stefano's wife, Claudia.

"Last year we tried, but we broke down after only a few miles. Quite heartbreaking," she says, and flashes a smile.

Stefano Ricci has helped keep the Panzeri family business going strong, but other silk companies have not been so lucky. In the past two decades, Como lost 80 percent of its textile trade to competition from China, according to *The Washington Post*. It was impossible to compete with the low labor costs in cities like Shengzhou, for instance, where work goes on around the clock to produce two-thirds of the world's neckties—that's two hundred million ties—most of which wholesale for between $1 and $5. At first, China's silk was cheap and of poor quality, but over time, as manufacturers acquired high-tech looms from Italy and Germany and honed their skills, their products improved. What they didn't have was European design talent, but they went after that, too. In one case, the Babei Textile Company, the largest of Shengzhou's 1,100 tie makers, collected a debt owed by a Como customer in the form of the Italian firm's design shop, "marrying," as the author James Kynge wrote in *China Shakes the World*, "hundreds of years of Italian creative tradition to the factory's ability to churn out three million ties a year. That is a combination that just might finish off Como."

At the same time, the cachet of the "Made in Italy" label was under siege on the home front. Starting in the late 1980s, thousands of entrepreneurial Chinese immigrants began arriving in Prato, a city near Florence with a long history of textile production. At first, they worked for Italian firms. But soon they began to set up their own companies, using cheap labor in the form of their fellow countrymen, many of whom were in Italy illegally. With inexpensive Chinese fabrics and designs swiped from current European collections, they turned out their own *pronto moda*, with a turnaround time of two weeks or less. The goods came with an almost impossible-to-deflect one-two punch: low Chinese prices and legitimate "Made in Italy" labels. With the production rate of a staggering one million items a day, the *Financial Times* noted in a 2010 report, "the Chinese garment makers of Prato could dress the world's population in 20 years." The apparel produced in the nearly four thousand factories was destined for both small vendors and well-known retailers, including fast-fashion giants Zara and H&M. The Bank of Italy estimated that in 2011 there was $1.5 million leaving Prato for China every day.

Meanwhile, the Italian-owned firms were hemorrhaging money and jobs: about half of Prato's textile makers went bust, and tensions between the two factions escalated. What seemed to annoy some Italians most, *The New York Times* noted, was that the Chinese were beating them at their own game—evading taxes, bending rules, and negotiating Italy's mystifying, often corrupt, bureaucracy. In June 2011, after a yearlong investigation, the police shut down 318 Chinese-owned Prato factories on suspicion of money laundering, tax fraud, and embezzlement. But there had been raids before, and the factories usually returned in the same locations, with different names.

Only the highest of the high-end, it seems—the Stefano Riccis, the Ermenegildo Zegnas, the Loro Pianas—have figured out how to stay out of the line of fire. Bolstered by the exploding luxury market in Asia and elsewhere, they have homed in on a marketing message that emphasizes quality, heritage. and the intangible Italian-ness of their brand. To survive, the Italians had to concede the mass market to Asia, and move on. In the process, of course, thousands of jobs disappeared.

"Going for the high-end is not good for the workforce," Richard D'Aveni, a professor at Dartmouth's Tuck School of Business and the author of *Beating the Commodity Trap,* told me. "It's good for artisans and designers, and for people with natural talent. But you can't hire the average guy who would normally be working on a production line."

"Be careful," Elisa says, as we step into the cluttered brick-floored dye room at La Polistampa, the family printing business run by her brother Giuliano out of a low dark-red building on the outskirts of Como. In the narrow kitchen-like space, numbered plastic pitchers of colored liquid are lined up on a paint-stained table. A young man is standing at a mixer, whipping up an intense royal blue. We pick our way around hoses and tubs and head into a long, open room that is filled with natural light from gridded windows. Narrow work surfaces run the length of the room, and on them, stretched tight, are yards and yards of white silk, like runners on banquet tables.

"This is where we print," Elisa says.

A burly bald man in a Torino Football Club T-shirt and a color-splattered canvas apron places a framed mesh screen on a section of silk in front of me. This is the pattern that was used to make the silk for Lambert's coat lining; Stefano had called ahead to make sure they showed me that one.

"He's the *capotavola*—the head of the table, the master," Elisa says.

"Each screen is for only one color." The man pours thick black pigment on the edge of the screen and then, with a partner, pulls a squeegee across the screen and back.

When the screen is lifted up, a pattern appears: a fine filigree of delicate black swirls. Another screen is laid down and the squeegee is pulled again, this time adding a flourish of dark blue. Then a third screen sprays a cobalt inside the black, and a fourth screen adds a touch of azure, while a fifth sprinkles fine white dots across the pattern. It is dazzling, the way the print builds in complexity and depth with each pull of the squeegee. I realize that I have never given even a passing thought to this simple truth: that printed cloth starts out as a solid.

Silk absorbs dye like no other fabric—but it is also delicate, and for centuries silk makers puzzled over how to tint the cloth without destroying it.

"Most designers do only three or four pigments in their prints," Elisa says. "Mr. Ricci uses eleven or twelve, sometimes more. We can only print two of these lengths—thirty-seven meters each—in a day."

I lean over for a closer look at the intricate pattern.

"Isn't it unbelievable?" Elisa says.

Raw silk is ecru, but Stefano Ricci always begins his prints on bright-white fabric. Perhaps he was inspired by Leonardo da Vinci's dictum: "For those colors which you wish to be beautiful, always first prepare a pure white ground."

"It costs double to get the white." Elisa shrugs. "But . . . he is Mr. Ricci," she says, rolling her r's with extra verve.

Back in Florence, I cross the Arno one morning on the Amerigo Vespucci Bridge. I am headed for the shaded alleys and sun-bleached plazas of the San Frediano neighborhood, where for hundreds of years artisans have been unlocking the doors to their workshops, picking up their tools, and going to work crafting beautiful things. I walk along Via Bartolini until I see a weathered metal plaque marking the entrance to the Antico Setificio Florentino, a silk factory established in the mid-eighteenth century by prominent Florentine families who decided to pool their personal looms and designs in a central location. On hand-operated machines, the weavers turned out fabrics sumptuous enough to grace the walls and windows of Florence's grandest homes. In the centuries that followed, bombs destroyed the factory roof and floodwaters ruined its archives, but the shuttles flew on, back and forth, like swimmers doing endless laps. Talk of the factory's demolition to make way for a hotel in the 1950s prompted Emilio Pucci, flush with the success of his iconic silk-jersey dress collection, to buy a controlling interest in the factory (his ancestors had been among the factory's founding families). But in 2010 the workshop was again on the blocks and facing abandonment. Stefano Ricci stepped in and rescued it.

"I buy that place for one reason," Stefano had told me. "Being Florentines since forever, we don't want it to disappear."

Stefano's plans for the Antico Setificio include restoring looms, bringing in a new generation of weavers, and perhaps starting a weaving school. For his fall 2011 collection, he also created a small group of shot-silk neckties, handwoven at the Antico Setificio.

It is easy to see why he thought this was a thing worth saving. Beyond the heavy wrought-iron gate, a stone path leads past old walls covered with gnarled wisteria to a small garden courtyard and a faded yellow building. An orange tree, heavy with fruit, and flower-filled terra-cotta urns, flank its red door. I am met by Douha Ahdab, the stylish young luxury apparel executive with an MBA and a résumé that includes stints with Calvin Klein and Escada, who has just been hired by Stefano. She shows me into the showroom, where rolls of jewel-toned fabrics—iridescent taffetas, complex brocades, and shimmering damasks—hang from wooden dowels and a basket of silk-pouch sachets scents the air with lavender and grass.

Douha leads me into the warping room. Here hand-dyed raw silk from Brazil, so fine it would snap in industrial looms, is being twisted into thread. A gray-haired woman in flat shoes stands watch as celery-green filament builds on bobbins. "Leonardo da Vinci designed that," Douha says, pointing to a corner and a tall, hooped thread-winding contraption, like a barrel without staves. We step into the main workroom, where a dozen towering eighteenth- and nineteenth-century looms sit under high-beamed ceilings. Douha has to shout above the steady clacking beat of weavers at work. To send weft through warp, they operate their machines by stepping on a foot pedal and pulling on a rope. We watch one woman working on a length of crimson-and-gold fabric.

"The cloth advances at only three inches an hour," Douha says. "And the pattern is so delicate that this weaver must stay with the length of cloth until it is complete; changing operators midway would alter the tension of the threads and change the look of the design."

In one corner of the room there is a Jacquard loom, which reads patterns off hand-punched cards, the way a player piano generates music from nubbed rolls. There are other looms that produce only silk fringe or Renaissance *ermesino*, a color-changing iridescent shot-silk taffeta that, if scrunched up, holds its shape like peaks of meringue.

"If you go the Uffizi Gallery, some of the women in the paintings are wearing silk that was woven here on these machines," Douha says. What was once used for apparel is now principally used in home décor, in palaces and estates all over the world. The Russian government is a longtime client: in 1848, the czar's interior designers came to the workshop for fabric to hang on the walls of the Kremlin, and more than 150 years later, when two great halls needed renovations, they came knocking again, this time for four thousand yards of silk. In the mailroom, I see rolls of celadon drapery fabric being readied for shipment; they were to be hung in a hall at Claridge's, the London hotel, Douha says, and had to arrive in time for the wedding of Prince William and Kate Middleton. Most of the fabrics, though, are destined for private homes.

"It's for a niche customer who has it all, who knows about beauty and quality," Douha says. "It's like haute couture for your house. This is the definition of 'luxury,' something no one else has. Some clients—especially in the Middle East—want it quick.

That's tricky. They always want things tomorrow. But this takes time."

Stefano Ricci is holding court at the head of a long table in a private dining room at Il Salviatino. Filippo had picked me up at my hotel and driven me back up to Fiesole for dinner with his family and a few friends. Seated across from me are a square-jawed Russian diplomat and his interior-decorator wife. Next to them are Niccolò, Stefano's movie-star-handsome older son, and his equally gorgeous girlfriend, who have come straight from the airport, having just arrived home from a vacation in the Maldives. At the other end of the table is Stefano's wife, Claudia, a serene moonfaced woman with bobbed Gloria Steinem hair, who oversees the production side of the company. On Stefano's left is a young man named Sedrak, who, if I understood correctly, is the son of the former president of Armenia. And next to me is the Milanese banker, the one from lunch the other day.

Stefano has the table rapt with a story about his wife's new car.

"Claudia saw one she liked, but we were buying other cars that day," he says. "Then it was her birthday—a significant birthday, I should say, and we were here having dinner in this room. And she was sitting here, with her back to the window, and all of a sudden we hear *vroom, vroom, vroom*. And the car, the one she wanted, drives up behind her." Stefano beams.

The dinner comes in waves—tiny plates of soft cheeses, shallow bowls of pasta, and platters of roasted meats. Over dessert, the Russian interior designer sets up a laptop and starts a slideshow of some of her Moscow decorating projects; each room is a lavish tone-on-tone explosion of textured drapes, shiny upholstery, fringed pillows, and crystal chandeliers. She keeps glancing nervously at Stefano.

"It is too long?" she asks. "Should I stop it?"

"No, no. It's fantastic," he says. "Keep going."

We linger. More wine is poured. There is a spirited discussion about plans to join in the culling of blue wildebeest in Namibia. There are passionate testimonials about the supremacy of Russian Standard vodka. The conversation makes me think of what Mary McCarthy said in *The Stones of Florence*—that this is a "manly" city. This is a manly crowd, with their safari camps and their liquor and their vroom-vroom cars and their singular brand of Italian swagger: J. Peterman meets Sergio Leone. And the thing is, I don't think I have ever met people who seem to be having a better time. I lean over toward the banker, whom I, encouraged by several glasses of velvety red wine, have begun to think of as my friend.

"It's nice to be a Ricci," I say.

The banker smiles. I think he understands.

"Stefano, he only lives one way," he says. "The best, the best, and the best. It's simple, really."

When dinner ends, there is a storm of cheek-kissing. I get back into Filippo's car. Stefano drives off ahead of us and peels around a corner with a squeal of tires. Filippo laughs and shakes his head.

"He's crazy," he says.

We make our way through the streets of Fiesole, heading back to the center of Florence.

"So, what will you do tomorrow?" Filippo asks.

"I thought I'd go to the Uffizi," I say. I want to see those women in silk.

"Oh, I can arrange it for you. My friend is the administrative director there. You won't have to wait in line. Go in the back door. Ask for Giovanni. He'll take care of you."

"You know everyone," I say.

"It's a small town."

We come across a bridge and ahead of us the façades of the medieval stone palazzos along the inky Arno River are illuminated in fans of *limoncello*-colored light.

"Ah. Look," he says.

I can hear the pride in Filippo's voice, as if he had a hand in designing this, too.

"Isn't it beautiful?"

CHAPTER 4

The Merchant

John Cutler already had pattern pieces for Keith Lambert in storage. These templates would be a solid place to start for the creation of an overcoat pattern. He went downstairs to the workroom and looked through the lightweight brown cardboard patterns he kept hanging in alphabetical order until he got to the L's. He pulled Lambert's from the rack.

Back upstairs, John unrolled a piece of fresh pattern cardboard on his worktable and pressed it flat with a warm iron. He then placed the back section of Lambert's existing jacket pattern on the cardboard and held it down with weights.

John consulted the notes he had made when Keith stopped in to be measured for the overcoat. Because the garment would have to fit over a suit, the tailor had asked Keith to keep his jacket on while he measured. The width of the back would have to be one to one and a half inches wider than the jacket; the sleeve length, half an inch past the jacket, with the hand held straight down. The "round" measurements—the chest, waist, and seat—had been determined in two ways. First, over the jacket, with two fingers inside the tape for a slight ease, then with the jacket off, adding two inches to the measurements taken over the shirt. If he had done it correctly, the second set of numbers would match the first.

John took his sharpened 2B lead pencil and, using the pattern piece as his guide, marked the center of the back. Then he ran the tape measure down to what would be the full length of the coat. He made pencil lines at the waistline and the chest, squaring them out for symmetry. He marked the width of the neck, then moved on to the shoulders, allowing for three-quarters of an inch fullness to be eased onto the shoulder in the making. This would allow the overcoat to pass smoothly over the shoulder blades. He calculated the crucial depth of scye—the depth of the armhole. Then, with a piece of flat tailor's chalk, he drew lines from neck point to shoulder end and then down to the scye and the waist. He continued, freehand, drawing a line down to the bottom of the coat. Then he removed the jacket pattern.

The tailor stood back and studied the result. Something was not quite right. He drew in a little more curve in the shoulder line—to add a bit of theater—then altered the shape of the side-seam line to put more ease in the waist. Finally, he added a fraction more across the back. Yes, that was it. He used his paper shears to cut out the pattern piece. He had the back.

He now turned to the front section and began marking it out: the neck point, the depth of scye, the waist. The length of the coat in the front would be one inch longer from waist to bottom than the back. He made some adjustments to the front edge, then drew a line from the front of the armhole down the full length of the pattern, making allowances to ensure that the coat would fall properly. He added half an inch to the side seam at the chest and waist, and three-quarters of an inch at the seat level, then drew the side-seam line from the chest, through the waist and the seat, and on to what would be the bottom edge of the coat.

He set the collar stand at one and a quarter inches, then made a line from there to the top button, six inches above the waistline. He marked the second button, and the spot where the lapel would break. The lapel edge, the armhole shape, and the underarm dart were all drawn in freehand. The welted side pocket was sketched in to accommodate the position, hang, and size of Keith's arm and hand. Then the bottom edge was joined in a soft curve from the front to the side seam. Everything looked right except the lapel. John made a slight change to the curve. That was better. He cut the pattern and set it aside.

Then it was on to the sleeve. The width of the cuff and sleeve was critical, of course, since the coat must slip easily over the jacket—but not be so wide as to appear sloppy. When he was satisfied, he cut out the sleeve pattern piece.

Now he was ready for the cloth. He spread the length of vicuña out on the cutting table and stood back to admire it. It really was extraordinary. John had acquired it in 1984, on the occasion of the firm's one-hundredth anniversary. Ashley Dormeuil, a principal in the Paris-based Dormeuil, one of the world's top merchants of premium cloth, was visiting some of his Australian accounts, as he did every two or three years. The tailor had a long relationship with Dormeuil; in the late 1960s, he had even worked at the company's London office for a time.

Ashley Dormeuil had given John a plaque to commemorate his firm's centennial, and had asked if there was anything else he could do for him. John had thought it over for a bit, then said that there was, in fact, something. He recalled that when he worked for Dormeuil there had been rolls of pure vicuña locked away in a vault. He asked if there might be any left. Ashley told him that he would see if he could unearth some. If he did, he said, he would be happy to sell it at a reasonable price. Ashley went back to Paris, and a few weeks later John received three long boxes in the mail. They were overcoat lengths of pure Dormeuil vicuña—one natural, one black, and one navy.

I pity the man who wants a coat so cheap that the man or woman who produces the cloth will starve in the process.

BENJAMIN HARRISON

On an overcast fall morning in Paris, Frédéric Dormeuil, a thirty-year-old executive with his family's luxury fabric business, is driving down the Avenue de New York and telling me a funny story about an experience he had with a Vietnamese tailor who tried to sell him counterfeit versions of his own Dormeuil cloth. This may not seem like the most amusing of topics, but in Frédéric's hands it is a one-act play *à deux*: the plummy Englishman meets the hard-selling Hoi An shop owner. Just as he reaches the climax, his cell phone buzzes and he checks the caller ID.

"Sorry," he says, then dives into a conversation in hyper-animated French.

While he talks, I look out the car window at the Eiffel Tower, looming industrial and gray above the Seine, and at the symmetry of the linden trees, their leaves like yellow paddles, which line the broad street. Frédéric hangs up and plunges back into the story: "And he was showing me the cloth—of course, he had no idea who I was or where I worked—and saying 'Nice, nice! Dor-may! Dor-may! Must buy!' And the name woven into the selvage of the fabric was Dormeuill—with *two* l's. I left him my business card." His phone buzzes again.

"Terribly sorry," he says. He glances from phone to road and back to phone, then props the device on the steering wheel and uses his thumbs to type and his fingers to drive. After he sends the text, he looks over at me, and says, "Now, where were we?"

Actually, I'm not so sure. I feel as if I've been around the world a few times since Frédéric picked me up at my small hotel near the Arc de Triomphe to drive me to Palaiseau, the Paris suburb where Dormeuil has its headquarters. Frédéric, who has the oblong face, ebbing hairline, lanky frame, and boarding-school elocution of a young British royal, is a whirlwind in a double-breasted suit. As the commercial director of Dormeuil Mode (his uncle, Dominic Dormeuil, is president), he handles all the international marketing, and oversees its just launched mens-wear line, which is already being sold in more than fifty countries. That means he travels almost nonstop. One week it's Shanghai for a trade fair, the next it's New Zealand to inspect the merino flocks, India for a luxury conference, New York for a salute to the tuxedo, São Paulo for a store opening.

"I once flew round-trip to Japan from Paris in a day," he tells me, changing lanes and speeding past a slow-moving truck. "That was a tough one."

His travels, I am quickly learning, have given him a wealth of material on which to unleash his Streep-ian linguistic skills, which he does repeatedly, with caffeinated gusto, as we head south.

Frédéric Dormeuil comes from a long line of indefatigable traveling salesmen. He is the sixth generation to hit the road for the company, which was founded in 1842 by his great-great-great-grandfather Jules Dormeuil, a twenty-two-year-old Frenchman with muttonchops, who had the idea of importing English wool to Paris. Encouraged by his early Channel-straddling success, Jules and the family members who soon joined him spun the globe and started packing. They loaded big leather cases with fabric samples—meltons, whipcords, cheviots, and serge—and lugged them onto railcars or ships bound for Yokohama, Casablanca, and beyond. When they arrived, they wrestled the trunks onto wheezing buses, or strapped them onto the backs of donkeys or camels, and set off in search of men and women who wanted clothes—and tailors who needed good cloth. They were sometimes away from home for years.

Dormeuil's headquarters, a boxy low-rise in an industrial park, gives no hint of the rigors—or romance—of the dusty road. It is not until I trail Frédéric through the lobby, past the low blond-wood tables and potted ferns, and down to the basement cutting room that I get a taste of that. Dormeuil's entire collection is stored here. There are miles of cloth woven with yarn spun from the world's great fluff: merino wool, cashmere, mohair, and vicuña. Near a bank of windows, a few men stand over unfurled cloth on long worktables, holding shears so oversized that they make me think of long-winded mayors and small-town ribbon-cutting ceremonies.

Woolen mills produce cloth in what are called pieces, seventy meters long, and one and a half meters wide, Frédéric tells me as we walk along the bins of rolled fabric. Almost all of the firm's cloth is woven and finished in West Yorkshire, England, which has been a center of textile manufacturing for centuries. Bulk buyers take the whole roll, but tailors need only small amounts at a time. They rely on merchants like Dormeuil to warehouse stock and provide a "cut length" service, from which they can order only what they need—generally, 3.2 meters, or roughly four yards, for a suit, less for jackets and trousers. Dormeuil cutters process about four hundred lengths every day, starting in the morning, with orders that have come in from Asia, the Middle East, Russia, and Europe, and finishing the day with requests from the United States.

"It's a real skill," Frédéric says. "You're holding these massive scissors, and every time you must cut perfectly straight lines through all kinds of different-textured materials, some of which are extremely expensive. You have to know what you are doing. Ideally, you should have a passion for it. But it's getting harder to find people who have the skills *and* the passion. I'm afraid the glamour of a local bar job can often be more tempting."

After the cloth is cut, it is packaged and shipped overnight to the customer. I take a look at the labels on four wrapped bundles on a cart close to me. They are headed to tailors in Milan, Azerbaijan, New York, and Tokyo.

Beyond the cutting tables are rows of tall metal library shelving. The company archives are preserved here, in hundreds of sample books. Some of the volumes are labeled in French, some in English: "Été 1889," "Winter Suitings 1914," "Ladies 1936." In one aisle, there are books devoted to blacks for mourning and whites for tennis. Frédéric takes a few volumes down from the shelves and brings them over to a table for me. Each lined page has a dozen or so small squares of cloth glued down its margin— some are frayed, some half-attached, some snipped back to nearly nothing. Next to the swatches are comments and numbered codes, written in flowing fountain-pen ink, indecipherable as hieroglyphics.

There are pages of solids and tweeds and florals. I linger over one array of sober charcoal-gray checks, which at first glance seem identical. But, looking closer, I see a thin vein of blue in the weft in one, a filament of maroon in the warp of another. Study any of these scraps long enough and each becomes an intricate grid, the careful work of one man who puzzled over the design for days before deciding that this line should bisect that one, unless, hang on . . . wouldn't it be that much better if they never met?

"Fantastic, aren't they?" Frédéric says. "People from couture houses pay us visits to see what we were doing in the nineteen-twenties or thirties, and costume designers working on period films come to make sure they get the look just right."

Dormeuil fabrics regularly appear on high-fashion runways—Chanel, Yves Saint Laurent, Dior, and Prada, to name a few, are all customers. The mills Dormeuil works with can do superluxury cloth in short runs, and respond quickly to the whims of designers.

"That's one of our great advantages. The Chinese mills make masses of meters," Frédéric says. "They can't do small batches. The couture side doesn't want big runs. Designer X will say, 'We only want twenty meters because we're making ten dresses, nothing else.'

"Sometimes we show a designer this season's collection, and he takes a look and says, 'Hmm. Change the stripe.' Or he will suddenly say, 'I want brown.' And we'll say, 'But the collection for this season, with regret, isn't offering brown. It's more of a blue theme.' And he'll say, 'No, it's brown. Since one minute ago.' We meet some fascinating people, very eccentric people. They change their minds, and if we want to stay in business, we have to move quickly."

Their contribution to haute couture generally goes uncredited.

"On the couture side, there are very big players—they don't need the name Dormeuil to sell," Frédéric goes on. "We'd love to say we made the cloth, but we're very much the back office with them. We have draped phenomenal people—presidents, actors. But we don't have the right to say it, because we aren't the final garment producer.

"Sometimes I will verbally let a trusted few know about who a certain fabric is going to. I'll say, 'That's for the Sheikh of X,' or 'Actor A is going to wear that in his next film.' It makes something that might be a bit dull for them more interesting. We made a suit for a well-known sportsman—it was a personal gift—and I told the ladies who were inspecting the cloth at the mill in England who it was for. They were thrilled."

Frédéric slips into a broad, glottal West Yorkshire accent to reenact their reaction.

" 'Oh, so 'ee'll be wearin' it, then? That's luhv-lay, luhv-lay.' "

Until a few years ago, when Dormeuil took over the Minova Mill in West Yorkshire, the company's goods had been produced to its specifications in independently owned mills. It was never content to be an anonymous supplier, however. After World War I, Dormeuil began to market its fabrics like Cognac or cologne, giving them catchy names and pushing them in print ads that were aimed not at tailors but at consumers. The firm also started having "Dormeuil" woven into the selvage of every fabric it distributed—a first in the textile world. By putting its name on the cloth, the firm took the limelight from the manufacturers and cemented its own status as a luxury brand.

In the archives are samples of the company's first big hit, a Scottish tweed called Sportex, which debuted in 1922. A heavy, plain weave of twisted wool, it was touted as being breathable, crease-resistant, and thornproof—just the thing for hunting, riding, and golf. (When the costume designer for Baz Luhrmann's remake of *The Great Gatsby* needed cloth for an accurate period wardrobe, she used Dormeuil's Sportex Vintage.)

With Sportex, Dormeuil pioneered not only the concept of apparel made specifically for active pursuits but also the idea that the endorsement of a famous athlete could help sell clothing. In 1934, it persuaded a promising and dapper young British golfer named Henry Cotton to wear Sportex apparel when he played in the British Open. Cotton won, setting a one-round course record of sixty-five in the process, and went on to become one of his generation's most celebrated golfers. Dormeuil recruited other top golfers to wear Sportex, as well as the French tennis superstars René Lacoste and Suzanne Lenglen, and the ski champion Émile Allais.

Print ads kept Sportex in the public eye through the forties, even as World War II limited the availability of wool for civilians. "If your tailor can't get Sportex—supplies are very limited— remember the name. You'll be glad you did when the days of peace and petrol come again," read one ad in a 1941 *Illustrated London News*. Postwar, Sportex took off. Dormeuil did four hundred versions of the cloth and adapted its marketing campaign, decade to decade, to mirror the times. The 1960s ads are period gems, featuring men with Austin Powers sideburns and wide-lapel plaid suits holding hunting rifles or leaning against sports cars next to leggy women in microminis. Sportex, one ad said, "was designed for men to get birds in sights or girls over barrels."

Dormeuil had another big success in Tonik, an iridescent suit fabric that was launched at a cocktail party at London's Park Lane Hotel in 1957. The cloth paired combed wool in the warp with angora-kid mohair in the weft. The natural sheen of the silky mohair was enhanced by being passed over a hot steel roller, which singed the surface. Tonik had a firm hand and was wrinkle-resistant—"like a bulletproof vest," according to one Tonik wearer. It became the fabric of choice for the slim suits worn by London mods and some of the era's most influential dressers: Frank Sinatra and his Rat Pack pals, Miles Davis, and Michael Caine, whose three-piece midnight-blue Tonik suit was almost a character unto itself in the 1971 cult film *Get Carter*. It didn't hurt that Dormeuil's provocative gender-bending Tonik ad campaign featured Veruschka, the six-foot-one Prussian, who was approaching the zenith of her supermodel fame. Dormeuil couldn't make the cloth fast enough—and mills everywhere raced to copy it. Eventually, the word "tonic"—spelled with a c—became a generic term for any fabric with that hip two-tone sheen.

I look over at the archives. Somewhere, buried in those hundreds of books and thousands of pages, there may be squares of the vicuña overcoat fabric that Ashley Dormeuil, Frédéric's late uncle, sold to John Cutler in 1984. Over months of emails, I had asked Frédéric if the cloth could be traced. I had the style numbers and pictures of the label. I wanted to know where it had been spun, which mill had woven it, and where it was finished. Frédéric tried, but it seemed that his uncle had left no record of the sale and told no one else about it. The origin of the vicuña cloth was a mystery.

There were mills on both sides of the Atlantic weaving vicuña—Worumbo in Lewiston, Maine, Stroock in New York, Northfield Mills in Vermont—but Dormeuil almost certainly would have stocked cloth only from U.K. mills.

Johnstons of Elgin, a Scottish firm that was an early pioneer in the spinning and weaving of vicuña, could have woven the cloth. James Johnston got his first delivery of Peruvian vicuña from a Glasgow wool broker in 1849. The fleece may have been smuggled out of Peru inside larger bales of alpaca. In any case, James Johnston wasn't impressed. "It turned out much coarser than I expected and was more difficult to work so that I shall lose money by it and not likely to try more," he wrote in a letter to his supplier. Eventually, he found a better source, and won a medal at the Great Exhibition in 1851 for his vicuña shawls.

There were other U.K. mills showing vicuña at that exhibition. The official catalog lists John and Abraham Bennett; Hargreave & Nussey; J. T. Clay & Sons; John Biddle; the Fownes Bothers; William Bliss; and Moxon, among others.

Pure vicuña cloth was not a specialty of Dormeuil's, but the supplier could get it for any customer who requested it—regardless of how he intended to use it. In a taped interview, a very dapper Ashley Dormeuil recalled a time in the early 1970s when a woman came into the Paris shop with an unusual request.

"She said, 'What is the best fabric you have?' I told her it was vicuña," Dormeuil recalled. "So, I said, 'What would you like it for? An overcoat, perhaps?' And she said, 'No, I want to put in on the backseat of my Rolls-Royce to ensure that my dogs will have a most comfortable ride. How much do you think I'll need?' "

Frédéric leads me upstairs to Dormeuil's showroom, where we stand over a round, flat black box embossed with gold lettering that reads DORMEUIL VANQUISH II. He lifts the cover off the box with a flourish, like a waiter raising the silver dome on a Wagyu rib eye. Inside is a sample of Dormeuil's top-of-the-line cloth, a blend of 60 percent Pashmina (the company's trademarked name for a very fine cashmere from Pashmina goats found in India's Ladakh region), 30 percent vicuña, and 10 percent musk ox, or qiviut. The cloth sells for $5,000 a yard, a reflection, in part, of the difficulty with which qiviut (which Dormeuil calls "Qiviuk") is harvested.

Each musk ox drops about six pounds of hair when it molts in the spring. Most qiviut is collected in the wild by nomads, who trail the herd and pick it, one wispy pennant at a time, from thorn bushes or rocks where it was snagged as a shedding animal passed by. Researchers have looked for more efficient and reliable ways to gather the fluff. In one experiment, giant combs were mounted to random boulders in Canada's Northwest Territory, in the hope that the animals might brush against them. This, alas, did not prove to be the boon to qiviut collectors that researchers had envisioned.

"It was hit or miss," admitted Sharon Katz, the inventor of the Muskomb, when I contacted her a few months after my visit to Dormeuil. "And the sites that were more reliably visited by the animals were far away from communities, which was not insurmountable, but . . . lowered the enthusiasm."

Collecting by hand, it takes about a year to get anything substantial, according to Frédéric.

"And even then we can only use ten to fifteen percent of what they have collected," he said. "Plus, the shortness of the qiviut fibers makes it extremely difficult to weave. That's why we only do ten percent."

Vanquish II isn't a huge seller, but it has served as an effective attention-getter among people who are attracted to over-the-top luxury. In 2009, the entrepreneur Alexander Amosu, who had made a fortune selling hip-hop ringtones and diamond-bedazzled cell phones, partnered with Dormeuil to create a Vanquish II suit. Stitched by hand with gold and platinum threads, and garnished with eighteen-karat gold and diamond buttons, it was sold to a British businessman for more than $100,000. Brioni also used

Vanquish II to make suits, which, without the precious gems, were a mere $43,000. The cloth generated a lot of publicity—and got what Dormeuil wanted: the attention of Russian, Indian, and Chinese tycoons who covet exotic, expensive cloth.

"There are customers who always want the latest 'super' cloth," Richard Anderson, a London tailor, told me later. Anderson is one of the new generation of Savile Row tailors and the author of *Bespoke: Savile Row Ripped and Smoothed*. He offers his clients both Vanquish II and Guanashina, another top-end Dormeuil cloth woven with a blend of kid pashmina, yearling cashmere, and South American baby guanaco, a camelid cousin to the vicuña whose fiber is almost as fine.

"And there are people who simply hear about something amazing and want it. A few years ago, for example, an airline magazine did a small piece on Guanashina and a new customer flew from Hong Kong to order two suits, with platinum buttons. He simply had to have them—regardless of price." Each suit cost roughly $30,000.

Dormeuil and other premium cloth makers never stop looking for ways to lure high rollers with exotic blends and appealing stories. Dormeuil recently began making a cloth called Jade, which is tumbled in the finishing process with powdered jade stone, a gem associated with good fortune in Asia. Scabal, one of Dormeuil's main competitors, weaves twenty-two-karat-gold threads into a suiting fabric. It also does a wool-silk blend woven with yarn that has been impregnated with microscopic diamond fragments, and another that has been pummeled with tiny bits of lapis lazuli. Scabal was also looking into weaving a cloth with platinum ore.

"Of course, there is the danger that the [exotic fabrics] appear too gimmicky," Michael Day, a Scabal designer, told me in an email. But, he added, the Chinese, Middle Easterners, and Russians, who are the biggest customers for the pricey blends, don't seem bothered by that.

Some bespoke customers aren't satisfied with what is available to the general public. They want custom-made clothing, produced with custom-made cloth.

"I had a customer who couldn't find a Prince of Wales check to his liking," Richard Anderson said. "It's a wonderful cloth, but nothing too special, since it's so popular and available in a wide range of fabrics. So we commissioned an exclusive pattern for him, with a beautiful green overcheck. He would have been the only man in the world wearing it, but he allowed five lengths to be made into suits for other Richard Anderson customers, creating a small club of 'brothers in check.' Perhaps this is true luxury—the ability to have something made for you that no one else, or only a few people closely linked to you, could have."

Cloth fiends can even have their name or other words woven into the pinstripe of their suit fabric. Scabal and Holland & Sherry both offer that service. Among those who have taken personalization to the extreme is Hosni Mubarak, whose suit stripe spelled out his name. Tom Benson, the owner of the New Orleans pro football team, has "New Orleans Saints" and "Super Bowl Champs" (a gift from his wife, who boldly counted on them taking the championship) woven in gold on his suit. Evander Holyfield has two custom cloth suits. One has pinstripes that spell out the words "The Champ" and the other says "The Champ Again."

William Halstead, a mill founded in 1875, even began offering a "design your own cloth service," in which it would produce enough fabric for just one suit using a hundred-year-old sample-making loom. The customer could commission any color, weight, pattern, and raw material—even pure vicuña—for his exclusive use.

Meanwhile, in order to supply the seemingly limitless appetite of the superrich for luxury cloth, fabric developers continue to search out new sources of fine fiber. Looking for an alternative to Chinese cashmere, for instance, Dormeuil reps trekked to Kyrgyzstan, a landlocked country in central Asia with a large goat population. Researchers had discovered that some herds living in remote areas of the Pamir Mountains, where crossbreeding had not occurred, were producing cashmere comparable to the highest quality found in China and Mongolia.

"The [farmers] always think of the local goats as being the bottom of the heap," said Carol Kerven of Odessa Centre, a research firm based in England, who oversaw the testing. "When we tell them that their goats produce some of the best cashmere in the world, their eyes become very big."

In order to help them collect the finest fiber, Kerven taught the herders to comb the fleece rather than shear it and showed them how to sort it for quality. In the past, the farmers had sold fleece unsorted by weight alone. Dormeuil uses what it calls Kyrgyz White in a collection of high-end suit fabrics.

Exotic fibers don't always catch on. In 2006, Scabal marketed a cloth made with Siberian ibex, or yangir, a wild mountain goat that inhabits the Mongolian highlands. Despite a promotional campaign that claimed it produced a cloth even softer than vicuña, yangir was a dud. The company abandoned the collection.

Cloth makers are looking beyond the animal kingdom for new sources of luxury fabric. In 2010, the Italian cloth maker Loro Piana introduced a linen-like cloth woven by hand from fibers extracted from giant lotus flowers that grow on Lake Inle, in southeast Burma. (The fibers had traditionally been used to weave robes for Buddhist monks, but the monks had to find a cheaper alternative.) Only a few hundred people in one lakeside community still have the skills required to extract and spin the fibers—tasks that must be done within twenty-four hours of pulling the plants up out of the mud. Two thousand stems are required to get a little more than a yard of fabric. Loro Piana committed to buying the community's entire production of about fifty-five yards a month, and paid in advance. The clothier sells lotus jackets in Europe for about $5,600. Because of trade sanctions with Burma, however, lotus-cloth apparel cannot be sold in the United States.

"The temptation is to keep looking elsewhere," Frédéric tells me. We have moved to a conference room surrounded by shelves of "bunches"—the swatch booklets showing Dormeuil's current collections. "We are always thinking, What can we mix? What can we play with? What is warm? What hangs well? What feels nice?

"But you also have to be careful not to take your eyes off the ball. We've nearly forgotten about wool. We have to reignite excitement about it, to let people know this wool comes from this farm . . . [to focus on] traceability and education. We haven't really done that, because we assumed people knew about it. It's just always been there."

Wool—whether from a sheep, an alpaca, or a vicuña—has much to recommend it. It is renewable (animals start regrowing fleece shortly after being sheared), non-flammable, absorbent, elastic, breathable, washable, durable, an effective shield against UV rays, and an efficient insulator that keeps the wearer warm in winter and cool in summer.

It is also biodegradable, an important feature when you consider what is happening in landfills all over the world. Pound for pound, we toss four times as many textiles in the trash today as we did in 1980. Thanks largely to the lure of constantly renewed inventory of cheap and trendy apparel in fast-fashion retailers such as H&M and Topshop, we buy more than twice as much clothes as we did in the mid-1990s. The explosion in disposable apparel has also made workers in the developing world vulnerable to sweatshop conditions and rivers polluted with dyes and pesticides. It's not just the factory towns that are being fouled. Researchers from University College Dublin found that polyester clothes shed toxic microscopic lint every time they go through the wash. The fibers were found on six continents where coastlines were tested; some beaches were more polyester fragments than they were sand.

Wool is mostly keratin, and it will break down. Polyester and nylon are petroleum-based and will be with us for a very long time. (Textile makers are developing polyester fabrics, trimmings, and zippers that are truly biodegradable.) But wool isn't perfect. As it decomposes, it releases methane, the greenhouse gas linked to climate change.

Textiles are among the most valuable recyclables. Preconsumer textile waste—that is, by-product materials from the textile, fiber, and cotton industries—can be recycled into new raw materials for the automotive, furniture, mattress, coarse-yarn, home-furnishings, paper, and other industries. Postconsumer waste from recovered textiles—even clothes that are stained or ripped—can be turned into rags and polishing cloths. Knitted or woven woolens can be broken down into fibers used for car insulation or seat stuffing. Other types of fabric can be reprocessed for upholstery, insulation, and building materials. Buttons and zippers can be stripped off garments for reuse.

Some agencies and businesses are trying to make it easier to recycle old clothes. In 2011, New York made donation bins available at apartment buildings all over the city, for the convenience of car-less residents, who would otherwise be tempted to toss old clothes into the trash.

The fast-fashion retailers have also tried to make amends—among them the world's largest retailer, H&M, which was lambasted in 2010 after trash bags full of unsold clothing that had been destroyed and rendered unwearable were discovered behind its Manhattan store. H&M has introduced collections of clothes made with recycled polyester and organic cotton. It also used fabric remnants for its collaboration with Lanvin to construct a limited collection called Waste. In May 2012, the store encouraged customers to bring in unwanted clothing of any brand name to donate to the Red Cross.

Marks & Spencer launched a campaign in 2012 called "Shwopping" in partnership with Oxfam, which encouraged shoppers to drop off an old item when they bought something new. The U.K. retailer hoped to recycle 350 million pieces of clothing a year. Patagonia, a leader in the reuse of textiles, partnered with eBay to sell used Patagonia gear as part of the Common Threads Initiative, in which shoppers were asked to take a pledge to buy less, repair what is broken or torn, sell what isn't wanted, and recycle everything else. Even Hermès got on the reuse bandwagon: the luxury manufacturer debuted a small collection called Petite H, featuring products made from leftover or rejected scraps of leather and silk.

Back in Paris, I don't see any recycled items in the Hermès store on Avenue George V. I do see many Chinese shoppers, with shopping lists in hand. I also see, at the end of the long glass display case, a salesman who has spread out half a dozen silk scarves in front of a middle-aged woman with gray blunt-cut hair. The woman is going through each one, holding it up to her neck, studying herself in the mirror. She goes back and forth, holding, considering, laying down one and picking up another.

"I don't know," I hear her say.

Now she seems to be favoring an equestrian print, now a bold floral. She goes back to the horses. I notice that her hands are shaking.

"I don't know."

The salesman is patient. I sense that he has been through this many times before. The woman picks up the scarves again, drapes first one, then another, around her neck.

"I can't decide," she says. This goes on for several more minutes.

"I am going to leave and go have a coffee," she says, finally. "I need to think."

"Yes, yes, madame. Go," the salesman says. "Think about it. Take some time."

I leave Hermès and walk up to the Champs-Élysées. I pass the new three-floor H&M flagship store, designed to blend in with the classic Haussmann architecture. (In 2007, planning officials had voted overwhelmingly to ban the store, saying the posh boulevard was being overrun by global chain stores and fast-food restaurants. H&M appealed—and won.) I walk through the crowds until I come to a Zara. I have been thinking that I need something to jazz up the simple gray shift dress (T. J. Maxx, rayon-polyester-spandex, made in China) I was planning to wear out to dinner with Frédéric. I browse around until a short motorcycle-style leather-like jacket catches my eye. It is edgy, I think, a little sassy. I am probably too old for it, but I'm feeling madcap and Parisian. And it really does look like leather, even though the label and the price tell me that it most definitely is not. It is—do I have to even say it?—a product of China. I think I look pretty good in it. The saleswoman agrees.

Back in my hotel room, I put on the gray dress and the new jacket, then head across the street to a tiny restaurant with red walls called La Cave Lanrezac. I find Frédéric sitting at the bar. He is impeccable in a navy pin-striped suit and a pale-pink shirt with white collar and cuffs. The proprietor seems to know him. They are conversing in French, pausing occasionally to purse their lips as they contemplate something that seems particularly perplexing, then blasting off again.

The restaurant has no wine list. Instead, diners are invited to walk down some back stairs to a basement wine cellar, from which they select their own bottle. I follow Frédéric down the narrow stone steps, and he finds what he wants right away.

Over dinner, we talk about Paris and clothes. I ask Frédéric if he can explain the difference between the feel of bespoke and the feel of off-the-rack.

"You know when you rent ski boots? Off-the-rack feels like that."

"Can you spot bespoke on people?"

"Oh, yes," he says. "Always. I always look."

I am pretty certain that he can also spot faux leather.

Later, when I am back in my room, I think about the woman in Hermès and the way her hands trembled as she touched the lovely silk scarves. She was overcome. Someday, I think, I would like to feel that way about buying a beautiful thing. In the morning, I do something I have never done before. I put the jacket back in the shopping bag, walk up Avenue Carnot, cut down into the tunnel under the Arc de Triomphe, and emerge on the

Champs-Élysées. I walk down to the Zara store, go in, and take the jacket up to the returns counter. I had kept the tags. The woman doesn't ask any questions, just takes the jacket from me, refunds my money, and smiles.

"*Merci,*" I say, and walk out of the store, feeling free.

CHAPTER 5

The Cloth

John inspected the vicuña cloth for any imperfections or damage. It was flawless. Then he took a hot iron and began to press it, using plenty of steam. This would remove the wrinkles and shrink the fabric so that no further shrinkage would occur in the process of making the coat. When it was ready, he began placing the pieces of the overcoat pattern on the cloth, making sure that they were all going to fit. He moved pieces around until he settled on a "lay"—the positioning of the pattern. He checked to ensure that all the sections were going in the same direction, with the pile of the fabric facing down. Then he checked one more time. It would be a disaster, a very expensive disaster, to cut any piece going against the nap.

Everything looked good. He anchored the pattern pieces with weights, and then took a fresh piece of tailor's chalk from the chalk box. He began to draw around each pattern section, at times using a gentle flowing touch and at times attacking the outline with the drama and flourish of an avant-garde painter.

He looked over the chalk lines. Satisfied, he did what he always did at this crucial point in the process. He ran his heavy cutting shears through his hair to capture the slight film of oil that made the blades move smoothly. Then he slid the shears into place on the cloth and began to cut.

To business that we love we rise betimes,
And go to't with delight.

WILLIAM SHAKESPEARE

I am in the heart of northern England's textile country, standing atop Emley Moor in the lifting fog of a cold November morning. It's hard to believe that not far from these open stone-fenced fields, with their constellations of grazing sheep and gates of moss-flocked wood, modern industry—in all its rattling, combustive beauty—was born. Engines changed everything about making cloth and about the lives of the people who made cloth—slowly at first, with many hands upon the odd new machines, then at a brisker pace, with fewer hands, until, at last, people were not much needed, except to push the Go button.

A post-breakfast walk has taken me to this green flank in the Pennine foothills above the River Colne and the valley that was ground zero for the Industrial Revolution. I had arrived by train the night before in Huddersfield, a big, blocky mill town about two hundred miles north of London that is to textiles what Detroit is to cars—both a symbol of entrepreneurial triumph and an emblem of sour decline. At Frédéric Dormeuil's suggestion, I'd taken a taxi out to a rural inn with a pub serving fresh Irish oysters and pints of Black Sheep Best Bitter. My room had a four-poster bed, blue-and-white toile wallpaper, knocking radiators, and long views of the moorlands.

I walk back to the inn to wait for Bryan Dolley, a fabric designer and consultant for Dormeuil, who has agreed to let me trail him as he makes his rounds from spinner to weaver to finisher. When the athletic-looking broad-faced sixty-year-old in a light-gray suit walks into the lobby, I am surprised by his sunniness and vigor. I was, I realize, expecting someone more out of the dark Victorian mill mold—stooped, perhaps, and with just a touch of consumption.

In Bryan's silver Jaguar, we head out of the hills on the narrow roads he knows well. He was, he tells me, raised in Huddersfield and never left.

"My mothers' side of the family were all local people, and nearly everyone worked in the mill—Crowthers Mill," he says. "My grandfather was a weaver, as were his predecessors as far back as I know. Everyone had to be at work at seven A.M. in those days. If you were late, they locked the gates at seven-ten, so you missed a full day's pay. The weavers all wore wooden clogs—I don't know why—and you could hear the stampede of feet at six-fifty-nine coming down the cobbled streets."

Bryan wanted to go to art school in London, but his final exam scores kept him from attending.

"I had a temporary job working in one of the mills at the time, so when my test results came through the mill boss said I should stay with them. That was the only career decision I ever made."

Bryan worked his way up the ranks and eventually started his own company, developing and selling premium cloth. His work has taken him around the world.

"I travel to see whoever has the money at the time," he says.

"Today, it's China, India, and Russia. Before that, it was the United States, Japan, the Middle East, and South America."

He also goes in search of the best raw materials for his clients.

"You can pick up the phone and call the commodity guy, but to actually go to New Zealand and pick out the best bales— totally traceable, even down to the sheep, which are numbered— I love that. It's a fantastic job."

As we drive, Bryan points out clusters of old weavers' cottages. He tells me about the old days, when cloth making was based in homes like these and everything was done by hand. Families got wool from their own sheep or from local brokers, then made what they needed and sold their surplus at a weekly market. On the ground floor of the stone houses, the women and children carded the wool to separate and straighten the fibers, then spun it into yarn. Upstairs, by large mullioned windows that provided the natural light needed for weaving, the men operated the heavy handlooms. When the pieces were done, they brought them to a local finisher, who washed the cloth in the soft, acidic water that ran down from the peaty hills. It was hard work, but, by most accounts, it was an agreeable way to live. Everyone was employed, and they made their own hours. The weavers were respected as skilled craftsmen and earned decent money. In warm weather, the women took their spinning wheels outside and the men tended to their gardens and animals.

A series of mid-eighteenth-century inventions changed all that. John Kay's flying shuttle allowed for the making of wider cloth, effectively doubling the productiveness of hand weavers. That increase in production spurred inventors to come up with devices that would also speed up the spinners' output. James Hargreaves introduced the spinning jenny, a contraption that made it possible for sixteen threads or more to be spun at once by a single person. Richard Arkwright's water frame, powered by fast-moving streams, could spin stronger threads than the jenny, at a more rapid pace. The spinning mule, invented by Samuel Crompton, produced even finer yarn a thousand times faster than previous machines. Both the water frame and the spinning mule were too large for home use, so small factories were built to house them. When Edmund Cartwright unveiled his power loom in 1785, operated first by water wheel and then by steam engine fueled by local coal, it ushered in an era of mass production and capitalist entrepreneurs.

"This valley was the perfect place for textiles," Bryan says. "It had the sheep and the soft water in the hills, and when the industry switched to steam it had the coal."

The cottage hand weavers and spinners, who sensed, correctly, that their jobs and their way of life were in jeopardy, did not welcome the machines. As Charlotte Brontë wrote in *Shirley*, the novel set in her native West Yorkshire during the dawn of the industrial age, the changes wrought by the new technology were nothing less than "the throes of a sort of moral earthquake . . . heaving under the hills of the northern counties."

Between 1810 and 1812, mills came under siege by mobs of angry textile workers, who came to be known as Luddites after a Robin Hood–like character named Ned Ludd, who had smashed two knitting machines in an unexplained huff in 1779. In Huddersfield and other mill towns, protesters ransacked factories, torched buildings, and raged against the machines.

"What loomed before them was not merely the factory but a whole factory system . . . with its long hours and incessant work and harsh supervision that reduced self-respecting artisans, with long traditions of autonomy and status, to dependent wage slaves,"

Kirkpatrick Sale wrote in *Rebels Against the Future: The Luddites and Their War on the Industrial Revolution.*

By the time the Luddite movement petered out, one mill owner and forty workers had died, fifty dissidents had been imprisoned or hanged, and dozens more had been exiled to Australia as convicts. And the machines marched on. Entire families, whole villages, walked down out of the hills and went to work in the factories. Children, some as young as four, who could fit into the tight, dangerous spaces behind and inside the machines to clean and service them, labored from five in the morning until seven-thirty or eight at night, sometimes later. When they showed signs of being tired, they were often beaten with a strap or hit on the head with a steel rod. Toxic dust fouled the air, and the rivers ran blue with dye.

"It was not our finest hour," Bryan says.

In the 1830s, child-labor laws came under scrutiny. Experts on both sides weighed in on the issue. One Scottish economist felt that factory life was not only suitable for children but beneficial. The mills were the children's "best and most important academies," he said, apparently with a straight face. "Besides taking the children out of harm's way, they have imbued them with regular, orderly and industrious habits."

But the grim facts suggested otherwise. The streets of Huddersfield were filled with boys and girls who had been crippled or made ill.

"Cooped up in a heated atmosphere, debarred the necessary exercise, remaining in one position for a series of hours, one set or system of muscles alone called into activity, it cannot be wondered at—that its effects are injurious to the physical growth of a child," P. Gaskell wrote in *The Manufacturing Population of England.* "Any man who has stood at twelve o'clock at the single narrow door-way, which serves as the place of exit for the hands employed in the great cotton-mills, must acknowledge, that an uglier set of men and women, of boys and girls, taking them in the mass, it would be impossible to congregate in a smaller compass."

There were some reforms made. The Factory Act of 1833 made it unlawful for children between the ages of nine and thirteen to work more than nine hours a day. But there was no going back: the factories were beasts that had to be fed.

"It is too late now to argue about the unwholesome nature of manufacturing employment. We have got a manufacturing population, and it must be employed," said John Charles Spencer, Lord Althorp (an ancestor of Princess Diana's), who fought against labor laws. "This is an evil that cannot be remedied."

By the mid-1800s, there were more than a thousand mills in West Yorkshire. To get the goods to the ports and the raw materials to the mills, train tracks had been laid and canals had been dug from Liverpool to Hull, following the valley floor or boring through the hills. Bleach and dye works were established to provide the chemicals needed to finish the goods. Engineering firms sprang up to fill the factories with machines and motors. Brick manufacturers churned out the blocks needed for houses, tunnels, viaducts, and more mills—always more mills.

When British sheep could not grow enough fleece to keep up with demand, buyers turned to Australia and New Zealand. And when plain wool seemed too ordinary, they looked to distant lands and more exotic creatures. Yorkshire winds carried cirrus wisps of fluff from Kashmir and Turkey and Peru, and in the mills spinners and weavers puzzled over how best to turn these odd, finicky fibers into cloth.

Some were young tinkerers who would go on to build empires. There was Joseph Dawson, a Bradford mill owner who, after a trip through India, where he had seen women using their hands to painstakingly separate coarse guard hairs from the valuable down of raw cashmere, went home and began experimenting with a machine that could perform the operation without damaging the fibers. Once he'd perfected the machine, he started the world's first commercial cashmere dehairing plant and launched the company that would dominate the cashmere industry for the next 150 years. His process was a secret known only to a few European cashmere processors until the 1970s.

Then there was mill owner Titus Salt, also of Bradford, who at the age of thirty found dozens of dusty bundles of alpaca wool in a Liverpool warehouse. The bales, which may have arrived as ballast, had been ignored because no one knew what was in them or what to do with it. On a hunch, Salt bought the bales and went to work. After a year of trial and error, he discovered that weaving the alpaca onto a cotton warp created wonderfully soft cloth. When Queen Victoria wore a dress of Salt-woven alpaca and Prince Albert donned an alpaca coat, demand exploded. Salt built four mills to keep up with orders and quickly became very rich—he even owned a private steam train.

The poor living and working conditions endured by textile workers and the foul air and filthy water in the factory valleys, however, had always bothered Salt. In 1851, he, by now sporting a long Father Time beard, bought land in the hills outside Bradford and began building a model village that he called Saltaire. A precursor to modern urban planning, the village had good housing, schools, a hospital, a concert hall, a library, and parklands. At its center was a palatial Italianate factory, the largest in Europe at the time, which at its peak employed some three thousand workers who wove eighteen miles of alpaca cloth a day.

Fortunes were made up and down the valley. Rolls-Royces clogged the broad cobbled streets of Huddersfield; every mill owner had one, with custom body and trim work done by Rippon of Yorkshire, the local coach maker, who could barely keep up with demand. For a time before World War I, there were more millionaires in nearby Bradford than anywhere else in the world. The fires of industry burned around the clock in this valley and the valleys beyond it, then spread to Europe, and America—in the riverside cities of the Northeast and the hill towns of the South—then to Russia and Japan.

"Here . . . in the Huddersfields of the north, our modern world was born," wrote James Morris (who would later become Jan Morris) in *The Road to Huddersfield: A Journey to Five Continents*, commissioned in 1963 by the World Bank. "These horny, stocky, taciturn people were the first to live by chemical energies, by steam, cogs, iron and engine grease, and the first in modern times to demonstrate the dynamism of the human condition. This is where by all the rules of heredity, the sputnik and moon-rocket were conceived. Baedeker may not recognize it, but this is one of history's crucibles."

Crucible or not, on this gray morning Huddersfield and its outskirts just look bleak. The yellowish grit stone used for most of the buildings gives off a jaundiced cast. Along the boggy river there are massive old mills capped with sawtooth rooflines. Some are abandoned and bombed-out-looking, their interiors scorched by arsonists and stripped bare by metal thieves. Others have been restored and converted into balconied apartments or offices, but even power-washed and propped up, the titanic Victorian mills still emanate a certain spectral gloom.

Yorkshire's reign as the wool-weaving capitol of the world lasted about a hundred years. By the mid-1900s, cheaper imports made by poorly paid and unskilled workers in Asia and Eastern Europe were flooding the market. At the same time, synthetic, petroleum-based fibers such as acrylic and polyester were promising better living—and less ironing—through chemistry.

"Cumbersome baggage will be a thing of the past, and businessmen carrying only briefcases will return from three-week trips looking as fresh as when they left home," raved a 1952 *Popular Science* article about state-of-the-art suits made of DuPont's wrinkle-free Dacron.

Meanwhile, the British mills were sitting on their hands, failing to update their technology, and fell further and further behind.

"The U.K. was a bit arrogant," Bryan says. "We thought we'd rule the world forever."

We pull into Slaithwaite—"*Sla-wit*," Bryan says, in the local dialect—a district in Huddersfield, with Victorian terraced houses and a navigable slot of canal running through the middle of town. Among people involved with the making of luxury clothing, Slaithwaite is known for one thing: it is the home of Spectrum Yarns, one of the world's premier wool spinners and the last such business left in the United Kingdom. Spectrum occupies a hulking hundred-year-old former cotton mill on the Huddersfield Narrow Canal.

"Here we are," Bryan says, still sunny, as he pulls up and parks in front of the five-story building, which is etched with soot and anchored by a tapered smokestack. Inside, I am introduced to Paul Holt, Spectrum's director of sales, who is clean-shaven and crisp in a yellow silk tie and a blue-and-white striped shirt. Under low ceilings hung with pipes and bars of fluorescent lights, Paul leads us through the factory. Spectrum specializes in yarn for worsted, the napless, tightly woven cloth that is used in apparel, especially fine men's and women's suits. (Bulkier and more textured "woolens" are made from fuzzy, loosely spun yarn.)

The cleaned and combed wool goes through eight separate processes before it emerges as spools of weavable yarn. On one floor, we pass wooden bins full of pillowy coiled wool "tops." On another level, dozens of industrial barrels are loaded with combed wool ropes called "rovings," which are waiting to be fed into machines that will draw the wool into ever-finer filament. On each floor, a few workers in blue coveralls and orange kneepads patrol the machinery.

Premium spinners like Spectrum do much more than shepherd wool into usable strands. They also develop complex, top-secret recipes of hues for yarns that will be exclusive to certain weavers and clothiers. In the high-stakes world of spinning and dyeing, blue cannot simply be blue. One of Spectrum's best navies, for instance, has seven different shades in it. Grays are twisted with bits of yellow and red. The blends give the final product richness and depth, but, equally important, they also make things difficult for would-be copiers.

"In China, there are huge mills with new machinery that is so sophisticated you don't need years of experience to operate it," Bryan says. "There is a green button and a red button. But they don't have the design skills, so they'll copy everything. These blends we make give them a big problem. We like that."

Still, China needs only about a month to decode and turn around a knocked-off design.

"We get one clear season," Bryan says.

To combat counterfeiting, some fabric makers, including Dormeuil, impregnate DNA into their fabrics to create a genetic fingerprint. A simple swab test shows if it is the real Yorkshire-made deal or a cheap imitation.

Paul takes us to a room full of spinning frames, which are winding dark-blue yarn onto hundreds of bobbins. Bryan walks over to one machine, flips a lever, pulls a spool off its holder, and studies it. Spectrum's machines look high-tech to me, but their technology, according to Paul, is intentionally less than state-of-the-art. Slower machines allow them to handle the most delicate fibers—even vicuña—and make single pieces for high-end clients.

"It takes time to make quality," Paul says, as he makes some adjustments to a reel. "Anyone can make the rubbish."

We stand and watch in silence for a while. I have no clue what is going on in the dark, unseeable reaches of these whirring machines, but there is something very pleasing about the way the spools are fattening up. On the way to the elevator, we pass a paned window, flecked with dirt. I stop and look out at a scene that, over the years, thousands of workers must have peered at. The mist has turned to rain, darkening the sepia walls of nearby mill buildings and creating brown puddles in the parking lot next to the old canal. Except for a single red truck and the green hills visible beyond the rooflines, the scene is as monotone and moody as a tintype.

Once we are downstairs, Paul says, "I have something you might want to see." He unlocks the door to an office. In the middle of the small room, on a worn cement floor, there is a giant clear plastic trash bag filled with what looks like brown stuffing.

Paul unties the top knot and opens the bag.

"Just got this in," he says.

I recognize the warm cinnamon color and airy clumps. It is a bag of vicuña fleece—nearly fifty pounds of it, Paul says, just arrived from Peru.

"That's about forty thousand dollars' worth. We'll use that up in about a year."

Bryan reaches in and pulls out a handful, and tells me I can do the same. I dip in with two hands and lift up a nest-size puff, being careful not to let any escape.

"When were you in Peru?" Bryan asks after we put the clumps back. He has picked up a tag attached to the bag.

"July," I say.

"Hmm," he says, studying coded information on the label. "Probably not."

That's okay. This may not be *my* vicuña, but I know the road it has traveled.

After Slaithwaite, we head north to Keighley—"*Keethley*"—an old mill town set cinematically at the confluence of the Rivers Aire and Worth. Above it is an amphitheater of gray-green moors, windswept and bleak enough to bring a lump to the throat of every English major, including me, as she passes through on her way to the Brontë sisters' homestead, just three miles away. Since the 1780s, this valley has been dominated by Dalton Mills, a sprawling stone complex with turrets and arched gateways, which, depending on the viewer's mood and the density of the cloud cover, could look like either a grand hotel or an asylum for the criminally insane. At its height in the mid to late nineteenth century, Dalton was Keighley's biggest employer, with two thousand people on its payroll. If you didn't work there, you worked at one of the thirty other mills or textile machine makers in the valley—or in the pubs and brothels that provided distraction from the monotony of the looms and the pervasive stink of privies and slaughterhouse offal.

By the 1980s, most of the mills had either been abandoned or demolished. Every now and then, a BBC or Bollywood film crew would show up to use the Dalton Victorian façades and loading docks to lend authenticity to their period productions, but for the most part the things that got attention in Keighley were not things to feel good about. There was the shuttering of Woolworths and the House of Books. There were the tensions between the locals and the growing population of Pakistani immigrants. There were gang wars over control of the heroin trade. And there was the disheartening, but not altogether unexpected, news that Keighley had been featured in a book of England's top fifty "crap towns."

Recently, though, there have been some signs that a pulse beats yet in old Keighley. The Dalton complex is being developed into residences and offices. (Abacus Bouncy Castle Hire and Premier Telecom Solutions have both set up shop there.) The clock in the mill's high tower is working again for the first time in twenty-five years. An ambitious master plan has been presented by investors, who envision transforming Keighley by 2020 into a town with a walkable and fully restored historic core.

And then there is the remarkable Pennine Weavers—the only working mill left in Keighley—and the reason we are here.

Bryan parks in front of a low building on the banks of the narrow, foliage-obscured North Beck. No one would guess that in this 130-year-old mill, which also houses a paintbrush manufacturer and a Royal Mail warehouse, some of the world's most valuable fabric is being woven—or that Gary Eastwood, a tall, square-jawed forty-two-year-old former local cricket champ and the mill's managing director, is a major player in haute couture and bespoke tailoring.

Pennine Weavers was founded as a small-commission weaving operation in 1970 as the town's traditional vertical worsted mills were closing down. Gary bought the company in 2003. From his small office, we can see through a window to the factory floor, where thirty automated looms produce about thirty-five thousand meters of fabric every week. This is superb cloth, destined for Burberry, Ralph Lauren, and Armani, among others—and for the cutting tables of the world's best tailors, including John Cutler and every top Savile Row artisan. Pennine does one hundred labor-intensive loom changes every week, prepping the machines to make short runs of expensive, niche fabrics, including cloth that is woven with twenty-two-karat gold and platinum. Dormeuil commissions half of the mill's output. This is where Vanquish II, the firm's delicate wool, musk ox, and vicuña concoction is woven.

"Vicuña is the most expensive fiber we weave," Gary says. "It's quite difficult to work with because the fibers are so short. Bryan has to buy up pretty much all the long-fiber vicuña he can to weave one or two pieces per year. And it's not the strongest yarn. Every time the yarn breaks and the loom stops, there is the potential for a mistake to be made. Vicuña stretches our people and our systems to the limit. Everyone gets a little nervous when they realize the value."

Bryan takes out a length of metallic thread that he has brought with him. It is pure silver plated onto brass.

"Do you think you can do something with that? In the weft?" he asks. Gary turns it over in his fingers, then calls another man in from an adjoining office.

"Bryan's got another challenge for you," he says with a laugh.

We put in earplugs and walk out onto the factory floor, where shuttleless looms are shooting weft yarn across warp. Bryan stops, puts on his glasses, and inspects the gray suit fabric emerging, one thread at a time, from one of the looms. The selvage identifies the cloth as Dormeuil's Amadeus, a silky lightweight wool that is the firm's best seller. He runs his hands across the breadth of it and regards it with something that looks very much like love.

Bryan, Gary, and I drive out of Keighley, up into the misted treeless moors of Oxenhope, where the Dog & Gun pub sits along a turn in the road. Inside, at a table near the fire, Gary tells me that he grew up in Huddersfield, the son of a man who worked in weaving.

"I guess it's in the genes," he says. "I started sweeping the floors in a mill when I was eighteen and got a degree in textile technology at night. Then I worked in a dyeing-and-finishing plant in India before I came back here."

Gary's biggest challenges are passing skills on through his workforce and attracting young people into the business.

"You've got to be prepared to work hard. But there are rewards," he says. "It's the whole thing about making things. You can't express yourself putting tins on supermarket shelves. We are making something. For all the ups and downs of the business, we're doing things here nobody else is doing. I tell the lads here that. They are making things here that no one else in the world can make."

Back in Huddersfield, we make a quick stop at Paragon Textiles, on a dingy block of low stone buildings. Paragon is the world's only commission pattern weaver that's still operating on traditional looms—some of which are more than a hundred years old. Bryan wants to see how a sample turned out—he's experimenting with yak. He finds the cloth, being slowly banged out by an old loom with giant exposed cogs. Bryan leans over and inspects a length of dark blue emerging from one loom. A cardboard box on the floor near it has YAK 10 PER CENT written in black felt-tip marker.

"It's like one of my children," Bryan says, above the noise of the looms. He looks pleased.

Most of Paragon's employees are close to retirement age, and the company desperately needs young workers to learn how to operate the machines. But a several-months-long search for two young workers willing to become apprentices had yielded no candidates. None—in a town where the unemployment rate among sixteen-to twenty-four-year-olds is nearly 21 percent.

We have one more stop to make. W. T. Johnson & Sons is a textile finisher run by fourth-generation brothers. Walter Johnson started the operation in Bankfield Mills in 1910 to make use of the soft Pennine water, the crucial ingredient in the process of turning woven cloth into something you would want to put on your body. I get out of the car and smell wet wool. Inside, there is a humid chaos of cogs and moving belts and hissing steam, like a train station in a noir film.

Nearly every premium cloth woven in the U.K. is put through Johnson's Rube Goldberg process of being soaked, scoured, pummeled, stretched, and dried. Without it, even the most expensive worsted cloth feels stiff as wallpaper. To move through the maze of machines, you have to step over narrow channels of moving water and pass open wells. This is the famed local water, filtered by layers of grit stone and shale, which is essential to Yorkshire wool-finishing. In the late 1930s, Johnson astutely decided that he needed his own supply: it took two years of drilling and a fifteen-hundred-foot bore hole to hit water.

Everywhere I look, cloth is rolling in and out of machines, folding onto itself like ribbon candy. Some of the machines are more than a hundred years old, like the one that scours and tenderizes stiff cloth by pulling it wet across wooden rollers. Others are boxy computer-driven units with blinking lights and monitor screens. Some churn out miles of cloth, others just one piece at a time. One passes the cloth across rows of teasels, prickly thistle-like pods that have been used since Roman times to lift nap.

Another shears away nap. One singes the cloth to give it sheen. That one tumbles cloth that contains fragments of precious gems. This machine beats on it until it looks old.

"Ralph Lauren loves that one," Bryan says.

Everywhere, there are tall stacks of folded cloth, on rolling dollies and on pallets, or draped over stands like layers of horse blankets. Bryan points out the selvage on one pile of black cloth, light enough for a suit coat. The words "100 percent pure vicuña" have been woven into the border. Most of what is stored here is in the business-suit color spectrum, but near the loading dock are stacked bolts of neon lime, intense red, and vivid purple.

"That's probably for Prada," Bryan tells me.

No one can be sure if the vicuña for Keith Lambert's coat was finished here. Nigel Birch, Johnson's product-development manager, tells me that it would have been a long process— probably ten to twelve weeks—from the time it arrived as raw fiber to the spinners until it was a finished fabric.

"It probably would have been scoured and milled, dried, raised, and drawn—probably on teasel gigs—dried, set by pot-boiling, dyed if it wasn't woven from dyed yarn, dried, redrawn, cut, brushed, and finally pressed—maybe cuttled and cramped," he explains.

Regular woven cloth, which comes off the loom feeling stiff, requires about two weeks to go through the twelve-step process of being cleaned, softened, pressed, and dried.

"The object, always, is to have the cloth feel like what it costs," Bryan says.

Each cloth demands a different treatment, and fabric developers are always experimenting with finishing recipes that will give them the end product they've dreamed about. One cloth will be washed on wood for thirty minutes, pressed for five, steamed for seven, go through two crops, re-steamed, and then put under heat. If it isn't quite what they wanted, they tweak the process. There are people here who spend all day feeling cloth—scrunching, rubbing, caressing—waiting for their hands to tell them they have it right.

Chinese finishers, on the other hand, don't have the time, or the expertise, yet, to experiment with cloth. What they do must be uniform, because they're doing so much of it at one time.

"Finishing is one of the few things that China can't do," Bryan says, letting his hand linger on a folded length of dark suiting cloth, before we head toward the door. "You have to be hands-on. It's like wine tasting. You can't invent a machine to do it."

CHAPTER 6

The Buttons

With the coat progressing nicely, it was time to consider the buttons. They, of course, were not to be taken lightly. The correct buttons spoke volumes, albeit sotto voce. They said, to those who understood such things, "This is a proper garment made with proper attention to details." Buttons mattered immensely.

There was never a question in John's mind about what kind of buttons to use for the vicuña coat. They simply must be crafted of water-buffalo horn. That was the only choice for a garment of this quality. Now it was a matter of selecting the color, size, and style.

John got out display cards that he had from Richard James Weldon, a London firm that had been supplying bespoke tailors since 1826. It was where one went for one's trimming needs—from kilt pins to collar meltons. He looked over the horn buttons. John preferred a matte finish, rather than shiny. More elegant, he thought. He pondered the color choices: navy or black. Navy would be the more subtle selection, blending, as it would, with the cloth. Keith, he felt certain, would prefer navy.

He chose eight of the size 23 for the cuffs, four for each side. The buttonholes on the sleeve would be real open holes. Some tailors made a fake hole for the top button, to allow for lengthening later on if the sleeves prove to be too short. John wasn't worried. He was certain the sleeves were the right length. He wanted size 40 for the three main front buttons. The button at the neck and the button in the center vent would be size 30, to avoid bulkiness.

John jotted down the style numbers. Richard James Weldon would no doubt source the buttons from James Grove & Sons, a manufacturer in England's West Midlands, which was considered the best horn-button maker in the world. No other buttons would do.

It is wonderful, is it not? that on that small pivot turns the fortune of such multitudes of men, women, and children, in so many parts of the world; that such industry, and so many fine faculties, should be brought out and exercised by so small a thing as the Button.

CHARLES DICKENS

"It is a bit peculiar," Peter Grove says as he steers his compact car through a roundabout on the way out of Birmingham on a sunny, cold November morning. The soft-spoken, bald sixty-three-year-old, wearing khakis and a raspberry crewneck sweater, seems puzzled by my visit, even after my many emails explaining my wish to see where the horn buttons John Cutler used to trim Keith Lambert's coat were made. I have the feeling, as we drive toward his factory in the suburban town of Halesowen, that he can't quite believe I actually turned up in the hotel lobby where we had arranged to meet this morning.

Halesowen—or "*Hells-own*," in the local dialect—is on no one's list of must-see snug English villages. It sprawls on the southwest edge of the Black Country, a coal-mining region in the low hills of the West Midlands. Settled in Saxon times, the town no doubt spent its first several hundred years picturesquely enough: fields golden with barley and wheat, pastures dotted with flocculent sheep and sturdy cattle, and woodlands full of fallow deer and meaty parasol mushrooms. There were half-timbered houses on the narrow lanes and, under a canopy of bent trees, the little River Stour burbled along cool and undisturbed, except for the occasional rise of a fish. The weekly market, held in the town center every Monday, was a carnival of hawkers pushing bread and eggs and freshly butchered pigs. By the late eighteenth century, though, Halesowen had become a very different place. Industry had arrived and brought with it the smoke and soot that, along with the veins of black coal in the ground, gave the region its name.

"The men, women, children, country and houses are all black . . . the grass is quite blasted and black," thirteen-year-old Princess Victoria wrote in her diary after passing through the area in 1832, five years before she took the throne. "The country is very desolate . . . engines flaming, coals, in abundance everywhere, smoking and burning coal heaps, intermingled with wretched huts and carts and little ragged children."

In *The Old Curiosity Shop*, published in 1841, Charles Dickens painted a similarly grim scene of a fictionalized Black Country town. "On every side, and far as the eye could see into the heavy distance, tall chimneys, crowding on each other, and presenting that endless repetition of the same dull, ugly form, which is the horror of oppressive dreams, poured out their plague of smoke, obscured the light, and made foul the melancholy air."

In those early days of manufacturing, the Black Country's men, women, and children labored into the night over back-yard anvils or in dismal foundries, shaping the bits that held the increasingly complex world together. They made bolts and rivets and springs and chains and anchors—including the three fifteen-ton ones for the *Titanic,* which, one local observer noted, were the only things on the ill-fated ship that actually worked.

Halesowen's biggest and, by all accounts, grimmest industry was nail making. Entire families worked in heat and filth, pounding nails out of hot iron rods. Every evening they trudged up Bundle Hill, where middlemen known as foggers were waiting to weigh and inspect the day's output. More often than not, the scales were rigged and the nailers' meager wages were paid in "truck"; that is, credit rather than cash, which was good only in overpriced pubs or shops that were owned by the foggers themselves.

When machines started to make the handmade nail obsolete, some of the people of Halesowen, including James Grove, Peter Grove's great-great-grandfather, went to work making buttons. James had an apprenticeship with Thomas Harris, who specialized in compression-molded buttons of animal horn and hoof. When Harris got into financial trouble, James left to open his own button factory in a rented timber-framed house in the center of Halesowen. He faced stiff competition. There were more than a hundred button makers in the Midlands, but James was a talented diesinker and a good businessman, and his operation flourished. Seven years later, he built a larger factory, at a site called Bloomfield, on Stourbridge Road.

Peter turns in to a driveway. Behind a heavy metal gate, I can see a new-looking building, blocky and featureless as a public storage facility. To the left of the entranceway, surrounded by a rusting wire fence interwoven with dead vines, are the last skeletal brick walls of Bloomfield Works, the old button factory built by James Grove. Most of it was recently demolished to make way for a modern plant that would meet safety codes.

The gutted old building's windows are spray-painted with

graffiti and the glass in its front door is shattered, as if it had been struck by a large rock thrown with ferocity. Just below the roofline, carved in stone relief, are four water-buffalo heads. Their horn-framed faces suggest nobility and power, even as they gaze down on the BP gas station across Stourbridge Road. It is impossible to look at the factory grounds and not be struck by how succinctly it telegraphs a twenty-first-century tale: the soulless modernity, the beautiful ruin.

"I hate it," Peter says as we walk into the new building. "The old factory had character. But we had no choice. We had to move or we would have closed."

In the small lobby, a table holds a shallow ceramic bowl full of buttons—mostly mottled brown disks and paler fang-shaped toggles, with a few coins of vivid color. On the wall, a framed photograph shows an aerial view of the old factory. It was a maze of narrow interconnected buildings with two smokestacks at its center, as dark and forbidding as an asylum.

"We had a ghost in the old place," Peter says as I follow him up a flight of stairs. "If you walked the factory at night, it seemed like there was someone behind you, but when you looked back no one was there. I didn't believe it till I felt it myself. It was quite eerie, really. I've been told the ghost will come back," he adds, with a bright note I interpret as hope.

On the second level of the building, there are several gray desks lined up near plate-glass windows that look down over the open hangar-like production room. I see a few men on the factory floor attending to rows of machines—some boxy, with modern-looking dials and controls, others that are hand-operated and appear old enough to be blackened with Victorian-era grease. At one end are two lines of large wooden barrels, spinning slowly like drums turning raffle tickets. And everywhere there are metal bins filled with brown disks—horn buttons in various stages of production. I ask Peter about the size of his staff.

"We are, at present, down to twenty-five."

"Down from?" I say.

"Six hundred, at our peak. When every button was made by hand."

No one knows exactly when or where the first buttons were made. Four- to five-thousand-year-old buttonlike objects have been unearthed in the Indus Valley, China, and ancient Rome, but they were likely used as ornaments, not as fasteners. Man found other ways to keep his clothes from flapping in the wind; heat-hardened thorns or sharpened slivers of animal leg bone, at first, then metal pins or nub-and-loop closures later. It wasn't until early in the thirteenth century that buttons with button-holes began to appear in European dress.

Historians can't say who cut that first little slit into fabric, tipped an anchored button through the opening, and felt it settle snug and fast against the two layers of cloth. One thing is certain, though: buttonholes changed everything.

"Buttonholes! There is something lively in the very idea of 'em," Laurence Sterne wrote in *The Life and Opinions of Tristram Shandy, Gentleman*. And there was. Thanks to the buttonhole, clothing became more than just draped fabric. Functional buttons allowed garments to be crafted so that they followed the contours of the body. The human shape, once concealed, was now visible and—with the help of a talented tailor—even enhanced. (The words "tailor," from *tailler*—"to cut"—and "button," from *bouter*—"to thrust"—appeared at about the same time.)

The change in clothing mirrored a societal shift as well. The collective focus was turning to the secular world, where outward appearances and the glory of the individual were to be celebrated above all. Buttons were also practical, providing a close fit that protected the wearer from cold. The historian Lynn White suggests that buttons even helped dramatically improve the infant-mortality rate during the Middle Ages—and, in general, played a part in changing parental attitudes toward children. At that time, some historians say, parents paid little attention to their very young offspring, because the emotional toll would be so great if the children died young, which they often did. White wrote that the development of functional buttonholes, along with knitting and crude heating devices, kept more little children alive—and helped foster modern attitudes toward them.

As functional, even lifesaving, as buttons may have been, they also quickly became both status symbols for the élite and an important new medium for artisans. Working in everything from bone to enamel and precious gems, members of button guilds turned out stunning miniature works of art. The finest buttons were reserved for the aristocracy. Sumptuary laws, which placed limits on who could spend and wear what, were enacted in order to protect guild members and to keep people from dressing above their station. Officials were allowed to search people's homes and arrest offenders who were in possession of the outlawed buttons.

Button fever raged among the sixteenth-century ruling class. In 1520, King Francis I of France, who was remarkable for his long nose, cutting wit, and preoccupation with tennis, ordered a black velvet suit trimmed with nearly fifteen thousand gold buttons for a meeting in Calais with his political and sartorial rival Henry VIII of England, who showed up similarly adorned with pearls and gems. A century later, Louis XIV spent $600,000 on buttons in one year—and a total of some $5 million during his reign. One of his coats was covered with fifteen hundred karats' worth of diamond buttons and diamond-trimmed buttonholes. People who saw him wearing the frock said that he sagged under the weight of it.

Buttons marched down front openings, across sleeves, around pockets, and along the back vents of men's coats—and if that wasn't enough, tailors would slash openings in garments for the sole purpose of creating more divides that could be bridged by buttons. In the mid and late 1700s, button mania peaked. The Comte d'Artois, who would later become King Charles X, used diamond-encrusted clocks as buttons. Other style-setters sported buttons featuring erotic etchings, insects under glass, or woven human hair. Some buttons were as big as sand dollars, others as tiny as lead shot. The most hopelessly obsessed changed their buttons several times a day. Some people found it to be too much to handle. An eighteenth-century English aristocrat's suicide note read simply, "All this buttoning and unbuttoning."

Buttons were just one manifestation of a change that was sweeping Europe. Before the eighteenth century, clothing denoted social class. None but the upper crust wore lustrous silks, ermine collars, and gold trims: it was easy to tell who was who. But the end of the feudal system meant that fashion no longer instantly conferred status. To make matters more confusing, faux jewels began to appear. Now almost anyone could get their hands on objects that only looked expensive. Paste stood in for diamonds, foil for silver, and gilt for gold.

It was a new social order "based not on birthright but on wealth, which was announced by extravagant display," according to Diana Epstein and Millicent Safro, the co-authors of *Buttons* and the co-founders of Tender Buttons, a New York City button boutique in a tiny Sixty-second Street brownstone that is considered one of the world's greatest troves. Paste and gilt "belonged to a world that admired surface over substance."

Eventually, men's fashions shifted away from the extravagant to the sedate. Color was out; earth tones were in. Horn buttons, with their subtle color variations and natural beauty, became the buttons of choice among tastemakers and custom tailors.

Animal horn was a wonder material. The world's first thermoplastic, it could be made pliable with heat and then pressed with designs or insignias, hammered into workable sheets, or powdered and melted down into a moldable goo. Sliced and pressed thin, horn was translucent as amber; leaves of it were used as panes for early lanterns—or lent-horns, as they were called in Old English.

Horn's major drawback was the revolting smell it gave off in the early stages of processing. Before it could be worked, the central pith had to be removed, and this was done by simply letting it rot away. In fifteenth-century London, which was already engulfed in human stink, rotting horn added a particularly vile note to the air—so foul that the Worshipful Company of Horners was banished to the outskirts of the city because of "the grete and corrupt stench" of their work. This, despite the fact that at least one physician believed that the fumes from rotting horn actually kept horners from "hyp, vapours and Lowness of Spirit, the common malady of England."

James Grove's horn came from domestic cattle at first, and then from more exotic livestock, including water buffalo and oxen from India, Russia, South America, and Africa. Great lumpy sacks of horn arrived by ship at the Liverpool or London docks, to be loaded onto carriages or into narrow canal boats for the trip to Halesowen, where they were piled high in outdoor storage sheds.

At first, all horn buttons were molded in hand-carved patterned dies. Later, craftsmen learned to split open and press the hollow section of the horn, producing flat plates, from which disks could be punched out. They also used the solid tips for toggle buttons. When the horn had been sorted by color and quality and cut into usable shapes, the leftover was ground down and mixed with powdered pigs' hooves (which gave off its own appalling smell) to make a nitrogen-rich fertilizer that was much in demand among English rose growers. Nothing was wasted.

James Grove's first big orders were for molded uniform buttons for both sides in the American Civil War—a coup that was dampened significantly by the fact that neither army ever paid for its buttons. Grove was able to bounce back from that disappointment in 1861, when Prince Albert died. Queen Victoria went into a mourning period that ended only with her death some forty years later. Naturally, her black attire and that of the masses who followed her sartorial lead required black buttons. Affluent women adorned their clothes with buttons of carved jet, but most found the semiprecious fossilized coal, mined from northern England, too expensive. James Grove figured out a way to make affordable jetlike buttons from compressed horn. The firm couldn't make them fast enough. The business expanded, and Grove hired more workers.

"There were probably five main families that worked here in the 1800s, then their offspring followed in their footsteps, and their offspring," Peter says. We are in a small conference room with windows that look out on the back of the brick row houses James Grove built for his employees. The descendants of James Grove were not, Peter admits, always the best of bosses.

"My grandfather, God rest his cotton socks, was a womanizer and a drinker. He was not a very nice person," he tells me. "Once some factory inspectors came and told him he didn't have enough toilets for the six hundred people who worked there, and he said, 'Sack two hundred people!' He lived on top of the hill, and he would have his horse saddled at five A.M. A lookout down at the factory would be watching for him. When he saw my grandfather riding down the hill, he would turn the gas lights down to let everyone know he was coming, and that they had to hurry up and get to the factory. They would close the gates, and if you were late you couldn't get in. So you lost a day's wages.

"In those days you'd also be docked pay for any mistakes you made, so people used to hide bad buttons in their pockets and throw them into the grass when they walked home. The field across from the factory was full of defective buttons."

Peter Harold James Grove was born in 1946. Until he was eighteen, his family lived in a spacious brick four-bedroom house in Hagley. In the mid-sixties, when the button business was booming, the Groves moved to the far grander Ismere Grange, a baronial gabled country house near Kidderminster. It had a swimming pool and long views of poppy fields and of the low hills of Clent. Peter's father made the seven-mile trip to the factory in a shiny blue Bentley.

"I was sent to boarding school at the age of six and a half," Peter says. "It was a very Victorian way of being brought up. I was absolutely terrified."

When he was home on holidays, he sometimes accompanied his father to the button factory.

"I'd go in on Saturdays to open the post with him. My father would open an envelope and say, 'Oh that's a nice order,' and then he'd look in another and there would be a check or an invoice inside. I got the idea of how a business ran.

"But I couldn't get close to him," Peter goes on. "He almost treated me like someone who worked in his factory. He had had a difficult childhood. My grandfather was very strict, and part of it rubbed off on my father and my uncle. We did have a very privileged life, though. We traveled in summer, took holidays to Europe.

"That was an adventure in the nineteen-fifties. The Bentley had to be craned into a hold on the ship to go across the Channel. Then we would go on these great drives. I remember stopping for wonderful picnics in France. When we would get to a hotel, the suitcases would be unloaded and people would stop and stare at the Bentley. Everywhere we went, people admired the car. And my father always looked smart. He wore custom shoes and tailor-made suits—always with our buttons, of course."

Peter joined the company when he was twenty-four.

"I had no formal training, I suppose, other than my father deciding at an early age that I would enter the family business. I first worked as an apprentice engineer at a German company, making button machines. Then I went back to Halesowen and learned everything about production."

By that time, Grove & Sons was making buttons for all the best Savile Row tailors and the top English brands: Burberry, Aquascutum, Daks Simpson, Marks & Spencer.

"They all had factories in England," Peter says. "Most of them either have closed down now or moved production to Asia. The biggest clothing manufacturer in the world was in Leeds. That's gone. We're just not making clothes in England anymore.

"We've lost all that expertise. And, once you lose it, it's gone. It's happening all over. I was in the Shetland Islands recently, where they are famous for their hand-knit sweaters—and everyone I saw making these beautiful garments was old. And they said, 'We don't know what will happen when we give it up. It will probably just die.' "

Grove's own children have no interest in becoming sixth-generation button makers. One is a firefighter, one is a physiotherapist, and one is in high-tech—"He's quite clever; he makes chips for these iPod things," Peter says.

I ask how it feels to know that he may be the last Grove to run the button factory.

"I suppose every family is disappointed when the [next generation] doesn't want to carry on. But there is no point in forcing them to do it. They won't survive. You have to have an interest in what you are doing," he says.

"I don't know what will happen. We may skip a generation. I do have a grandson. I can put the business in trust."

By that time, though, the mysteries of working with animal horn may have died with Peter Grove.

"I am the only one here who knows anything about the character of horn," he says. "I grew up with it, you see. I think a lot of it is knowledge you can't pass on. There are very few of us left."

"That's sad," I say.

" 'Tis. 'Tis sad."

Outside the door to the factory floor, Peter hands me protective safety gear—government regulations.

"I hate that I have to put on glasses and earplugs before I go into my own factory," he says, blinking through oversized clear goggles. "I feel like a bloody freak."

Once inside, I can still hear the banging of the barrels and the whine of a saw. There are buttons in various stages of production everywhere, in bins and carts and barrels. One container holds stag-horn ovals, their brown-ridged surfaces rough as bark.

Another is filled with dark shiny toggles. Nearby is a bin filled with buttons with ridged perimeters, about the size and shape of the ones on Keith Lambert's coat.

"I think these are like the ones on the vicuña coat," I shout to Peter above the din.

He picks up one of the disks.

"It takes five weeks to make a button like that," he shouts back.

I look around the room and picture Keith Lambert's buttons moving, cartoon-like, through the production chain—first turned, then drilled, tumbled, dyed, lacquered, dried, and then, at last, buffed to a lovely soft finish—with just enough sheen to catch the light, but not so much as to bounce it back.

In the next room, we are allowed to take off the safety glasses and remove the earbuds. Here aisles of shelving hold bins filled with button blanks—dusty-looking wafers sent from India that have been punched out of bone and horn and hoof.

"This is how we do it now," Peter says, holding up a disk that is grained with power-saw marks. "We don't deal with the whole horn anymore."

In another small room, three women are working at metal tables, picking up buttons one at a time, and sorting them by natural color.

"Sorting is our real expertise," Peter says with satisfaction.

We watch the women group buttons that will be part of matched sets, then I follow Peter into an adjacent room, which is filled with dye vats. This must be where Keith Lambert's buttons were dyed navy blue.

"It's very tricky dyeing a natural product," Peter says. "It's not an exact science. There is a grain to horn. One batch works, one doesn't. We are the only ones who ever figured out how to dye it black."

I raise my camera in front of one of the vats.

"Oh, you can't take pictures of that," Peter says quickly. "Secret formula."

We move into a narrow storage area, which has floor-to-ceiling shelves filled with row upon row of small cardboard boxes. Every box has a handwritten description on it. Some of the names are familiar brands (Burberry, John Lewis, Jaeger). Others whisper of mist and heathlands (Cotswold, Balmoral, Windsmoor) or intrigue (Sabotage), or even redemption (Reforma). Still others (Sticky Finger and Hot Rockin') hint of buttons that were designed chiefly to be undone.

In another small room, two women sit in straight-backed chairs placing buttons, one by one, on trays painted with a grid like a giant checkerboard. When they have completed a board, they slide it carefully onto a cart. Once the cart is filled, it will be wheeled into another area for the next phase, the spraying of lacquer. I can smell the acetone bite in the air.

"A lot of places, the buttons come off [the production line] and go into a box," Peter says. "But we do one-hundred-percent inspection. It's our reputation on the line. If we do get a complaint—and it doesn't happen very often—we take it seriously. You have to instill in the people that work here that what we make is a quality product. And they are all of that mind. They won't say, 'That will do.' "

I ask him what else sets his buttons apart from others.

"The character of the person who makes it—it's built right into the button. Our buttons are the best in the world."

I follow him back through a bright room close to the front entry.

"This is where I hope to have the button museum," Peter says. "Eventually."

On the walls there are already several framed sixties-era black-and-white photographs, gauzy and evocative as balladeer album covers. In one, natural light streams in on a line of women sorting buttons in front of shiny metal funnels. In another, a group, again mostly women, are walking through the factory gates, coiffed and smiling, as if they might be headed for a Petula Clark concert rather than getting off a long shift. Peter lingers over the pictures.

"They were great old days."

In that era, the luxury brands always wanted quality horn buttons on their garments. Then, looking for places to cut costs, they began to scrimp and went with plastic—or they found cheaper versions of horn.

"There are others who do horn—in India, for instance, but their quality is absolutely appalling," Peter continues. "We build a shape into ours, with corners and definite lines. Our competitors' buttons are wishy-washy. They take the easy way, and we take the more difficult way, to produce a better button. A good horn button takes time."

These days, Grove's main trade is with the niche world of high-end tailoring. Grove buttons adorn the garments of the powerful and the famous.

"Prince Charles's suits would have our buttons on them, but we can't say it," Peter tells me. "Buttons are the ass-end of the clothing business."

Bespoke tailors, such as Anderson & Sheppard in London, view Grove's buttons as the best. David Walters, the head trimmer, who is in charge of securing buttons for all the firm's garments, told me in an email that he has to explain to his customers that horn buttons are one of a kind and can enhance the beauty of a garment.

"We educate and guide them towards understanding," he said. "Most [clients] have been brought up in a mass-produced era where the button is simply a tool to fasten their garment together."

The truth, of course, is that most of the world's buttons are simply that. They have not been hand-sorted for subtleties of tone and grain or inspected for uniformity of sheen and hue. They are likely wafers of cheap polyester resin, sometimes cut with chalk filler and prone to breakage under the weight of a dry-cleaning press or in the battering chaos of a washing machine. And there is a very high probability that they were made in Qiaotou, an industrial boomtown in southeast China that in the past thirty years has become the center of the button universe.

Qiaotou—you know you have arrived when you see the twenty-foot-high silver statue of a winged button—produces fifteen billion buttons a year, or about two-thirds of the world's button needs. In the thirty years since local factories made their first buttons, the town went from agricultural backwater to industrial juggernaut—and, along the way, wiped out most of the international competition.

Qiaotou's ascension to button supremacy began, as the story goes, in 1980 when two brothers found some discarded buttons in the street and set up a stand to sell them. Spurred by the brothers' success, other families began selling, and then manufacturing, buttons.

"Buttons turned out to be a growth industry in the nineteen-eighties, in part because many Chinese entered the decade with just a couple of Mao tunics to their name and ended it with a wardrobe full of shirts," Nicholas Kristof wrote in a 1993 *New York Times* report on China's button boom.

Button making—and then zipper making—exploded in Qiaotou, thanks to the backing of European apparel makers who were eager to cut costs and a population willing to work for peanuts and overlook the grim environmental fallout of plastics manufacturing. By 2005, the town, known as Button City, had some seven hundred factories and owned the international fastener market. Even Grove thought about moving some of its production offshore.

"We looked at going to China," Peter admits. "But that was a no, because they take all your technology and throw you out. Then we thought we might build a factory in India, but in actual fact we couldn't produce much cheaper than what we do here, because the costs of starting a business there were colossal. Not just the cost of putting up the factory. It's all the bloody bribes. We were talking to one chap near a piece of ground in Bangalore, and he said if we go through the proper channels it would take two years. But, he said, 'I know the man—if you bribe him, it will take four weeks.' Even now, some of the materials we buy in India, we have to bribe people. With all the red tape to get licenses, you have to cross somebody's palm with a bit of money."

The mass production of cheap buttons makes Peter Grove queasy.

"Anyone can make millions of buttons with no character," he says.

I look down at the flimsy plastic buttons on my cardigan and feel a little guilty for never having given my buttons credit for even having the potential for character—or, really, ever having given them any thought at all.

There is a population of people, it turns out, who think a great deal about buttons—more, in fact, than might be deemed entirely healthy. These people are competitive button collectors, most of whom are members of either the U.S.-based National Button Society or the U.K.'s British Button Society. Their thousands of members spend most of their time buying, trading, selling, and researching buttons. Several times a year, they gather at conventions to enter their button collections in contests. Their entries are displayed on what are known as trays—nine-by-twelve-inch display cards on which collections have been painstakingly curated by color or material or theme in accordance with the button societies' strict classification rules. Some collectors get obsessed with a certain design—birds, for instance—and spend years, or even decades, on the hunt for avian fasteners to complete a set or create a compelling tray presentation.

"The set was the scorecard," Steven Gelber wrote in *Hobbies: Leisure and the Culture of Work in America.* "Collectors had to impose some pattern on their acquisition so they could know not only what they had but also what they did not have. Creating an arbitrary series so that one could then fill it is, no doubt, odd behavior in the eyes of those who do not share the hobby but it is how the game is played."

Button collecting is not new. The earliest button collectors were young women, who, just after the Civil War, began making "charm strings" that they believed would bring them luck in love. No string could have two of the same buttons, a requirement that led, according to an 1898 account in *The American Archaeologist,* to a rash of button thefts: "It was not uncommon while that craze lasted for garments to be entirely stripped of their buttons by pestiferous collectors."

The fad—and the pilfering—faded away for a time, but button collecting resurfaced in 1938, when a New Jersey housewife named Gertrude Patterson appeared on a popular radio show to talk about her button collection. The show, called *Hobby Lobby*, was hosted by Dave Elman, a vaudeville performer and hypnotist, who conceived of the broadcast as a way "to tell the troubled world how to dispel gloom by making better use of its free time."

Gertrude Patterson's appearance sent radio listeners across the country racing up to their attics in search of their grandmother's button jars. In January 1939, *Hobbies* magazine announced the formation of the National Button Society, and later that year, *Ladies' Home Journal* ran an article encouraging women to take up button collecting in order to "become more charming and beautiful."

Men were urged to embrace the hobby as well. *The Complete Button Book*, written in 1949 by Lillian Smith Albert and Kathryn Kent, reminded reluctant would-be male collectors that buttons could be manly: "Nearly two thirds of buttons made before 1820 were made for the use of that once proud peacock, the male of the species. Kidd, the pirate, wore buttons of silver and gold."

Men did get interested, but only when button collecting became commodified.

"The absurdity of collecting inherently low-value products disappeared when collecting became a process that turned garbage into gold," according to Gelber.

There was, and still is, some money to be made. Nineteenth-century compressed horn buttons featuring the Swedish opera singer Jenny Lind can go for about $100 each. Vintage French enamels sell for hundreds of dollars; buttons from the uniforms of Confederate soldiers sell for thousands. And in 2000, a rare lacy glass button in the shape of an ear of corn sold for $12,000. Most collectors, however, are drawn to buttons not for their cash value but for their implied backstory—for the way they offer a small but powerful connection to the past. As Martha Stewart, who knows a thing or two about collections, said, "Buttons are the fossils of the sartorial world."

Charles de Gaulle collected buttons from French army uniforms. Jacqueline Kennedy Onassis went for rare French enamels. Buttons from the eighteenth century captivated Baroness Edmond de Rothschild. Margaret Woodbury Strong, an heir to the Eastman Kodak fortune, bought them by the bushelful.

Some people fall into collecting buttons when they inherit a stash from an elderly relative—sometimes just a mayonnaise jar full of buttons, sometimes a much more elaborately curated collection. Jocelyn Howells, a past president of the National Button Society and one of the button world's queen bees, started with a collection that had been carefully classified and mounted by her grandmother. She now has a million and a half buttons, the value of which—well, she would rather not say.

"Anyone who knows anything about buttons today will know, with that many buttons, it would add up to a lot," Jocelyn said when I spoke to her by telephone. She seemed like a rational and pleasant person, though she did get a little worked up as she told me a story about an acquaintance who tried to wangle one of her prized buttons away from her in a questionable deal. Her tale hints at the darker path collectors sometimes find themselves walking down.

The most predatory button collectors carry small scissors to nip buttons off garments left unattended or hanging on racks. Felicidad Noriega, the wife of Manuel Noriega, was arrested in 1991 for cutting twenty-seven buttons off apparel at a Burdines department store in Miami. (She agreed to a plea bargain, paid restitution, and performed a hundred hours of community service.) At a Macy's store, salesclerks in the designer-apparel department were puzzled by clothes that had been stripped of their buttons. Security personnel stepped up their surveillance and eventually identified the perp—she was a sweet-faced, gray-haired woman in a wheelchair, who could be seen on surveillance tape rolling from rack to rack, scissors in hand.

Chanel's double "C" logo buttons are particularly tempting targets. Simon Doonan, creative director for Barneys, recalled hearing a story about a woman who took a Chanel suit into a fitting room, cut off the buttons, and inserted them into her vagina. Security personnel recovered the loot by handing her a bowl and waiting outside the fitting room. Freida Warther spent eighty-three years amassing the seventy-three thousand buttons that covered the walls and ceiling of her house in intricate patterns, now open to the public at the Warther Museum in Dover, Ohio. A die-hard collector to the end, she had, it was discovered, been cutting off the buttons of her nurse's London Fog raincoat from her nursing-home bed.

Most collectors do not go to such extremes, but they are serious about their buttons. They attend conventions armed with magnifying glasses used to scrutinize and identify possible purchases. They know that a button made of bone will show tiny black specks where the blood traveled through; ivory will show crosshatch lines. Horn buttons can be identified by pick marks—the small holes were gouged into the backs of the buttons when they were plucked out of the mold.

Collectors also use needles, heated with lighters or matches, to identify materials. Burning the button produces certain signature odors. According to the National Button Society, jet smells like coal gas; Lucite like nail-polisher remover; tortoiseshell like stagnant salt water; and vegetable ivory like burning walnut shells. Horn smells of cooking meat or burning feathers.

It's more than curiosity that drives collectors to accurately identify what a button is made of. Celluloid, the world's first semi-synthetic plastic, was used as a stand-in for ivory, tortoiseshell, jade, and marble until it became widely known that it was highly flammable. An 1892 issue of *Chemist + Druggist* recounted a case in which a woman was burned when she was standing by a fireplace and her buttons ignited. (Motion-picture film was made of celluloid until a series of fatal theater fires caused by the combustion of film made it obvious that a different material needed to be used.) For collectors, celluloid poses another problem: the material has a tendency to self-destruct if closed up in airtight containers, committing what is known in button circles as celluloid suicide.

Other materials caught on for a while, and then faded away. In the early 1900s, one in every five buttons produced in the United States was made of tagua, a golf-ball-size nut that grows on palm trees on the northwestern coast of South America. The nuts, which arrived as ballast on ships, were cheaper than ceramic or metal and were hard and white as ivory once they were dried. Tagua buttons were used extensively on World War I uniforms. This seemed a fine idea until troops discovered that trench rats had a taste for the nuts and gnawed them off their pants. A movement toward natural sustainable products spurred renewed interest in tagua fasteners. In the late 1980s Patagonia, the outdoor-apparel maker, replaced plastic buttons with rain-forest tagua-nut buttons, but was swamped with returns when customers discovered that the nuts disintegrated in the washing machine.

Pearl buttons, made from the iridescent lining of fresh-and salt-water shells, were popular in the late 1800s and early 1900s, and for several decades Muscatine, Iowa, which harvested mussel shells from the Missouri River, thrived as the "Pearl Button Capitol of the World." By the 1960s, however, the industry was all but dead—and so was Muscatine.

At about the same time, the horn-button industry and the town of Halesowen went into precipitous decline. The trains stopped running. The brick rail station that stood at the foot of Mucklow Hill, with its potted flowers and ivy-covered façade, was torn down. And the majestic hundred-foot-high viaduct that spanned Dowery Dell was demolished.

I ask Peter if he could show me Halesowen.

"Nothing to see, really. It's a bit of a ghost town now."

I tell him I would still like to see it, so we go out to his car and drive through the factory gates. We pass the Waggon & Horses, a corner pub with sloping floors and church-pew benches, where not much has changed since the 1800s—except for the fact that, a few years back, it started charging for the gherkins that had always come free with the turkey-and-ham pie.

"Spit and sawdust," Peter says. "You don't want to go in there."

Ahead, I can see the spiky tower of the St. John the Baptist Church. Built of dark mottled sandstone cut from local quarries, the nine-hundred-year-old Norman church has nearly always been the thing to look for in finding your way home from the hamlets around Halesowen—from Cakemore and Lutley and Warley Wigorn, and beyond. We park nearby and walk to the churchyard. There is a large cemetery behind an iron fence where dry brown leaves have eddied around the old mossy gravestones. James Grove and seventy-five other members of the extended Grove family are buried here. Inside the church, one of the tall stained-glass windows is dedicated to James Grove, hinting at the stature of the family and the near-sanctity of the button in this town.

"You don't want to go in, do you?" Peter says.

We walk a few blocks to the center of town, where there is a new bus station, a modern-looking silver-and-royal-blue structure that looks out of place. Beyond the station is an ASDA, the Walmart-owned U.K. superstore, and the entrance to the Cornbow covered shopping center. The downtown mall is the legacy of a 1950s decision by town officials to raze Halesowen's commercial heart and start over. That the mayor at the time, Peter William Scott, was a demolition contractor and the councilmen were all builders are facts that have not been lost on critics who mourn the flattening of the town's historic core.

"It used to be a lovely old high street, filled with family businesses," Peter says.

There was Sidney Shacklock's haberdashery, W. S. Welch's drapery shop, Wrensons grocery, W. Hollies butcher shop. The buildings were replaced with boxy structures capped with cement overhangs that seem designed to block any rogue ray of sun that might have escaped through the Midlands cloud clover. In 1968, the main shopping streets were pedestrianized and the area was christened "the Precinct," a name that cleverly presaged the need to step up police presence in the long, dark tunnel that led to the shops and became a favorite hangout of drug dealers and teenage thugs. In the eighties, a roof was constructed over the strip to create an indoor mall.

For a short time, the town perked up—until, that is, the opening of the Merry Hill Shopping Centre about five miles away. There was free parking for ten thousand cars, two hundred shops, a ten-screen cinema, England's first drive-through McDonald's, and a monorail—a monorail!—to whisk shoppers from their cars. (Enthusiasm for the futuristic train withered when twenty passengers had to be rescued after spending hours fifty feet above ground in a disabled train—in what newspapers called the "Merry Hill Train Terror.") The monorail shut down in 1996, but the shopping center grew, attracting retail giants like H&M, Debenhams, the Disney Store, Gap, and Marks & Spencer. Best Buy and Staples opened nearby. Halesowen—and the other towns around the mall—didn't have a prayer.

In the bluish light of the Cornbow Center, Peter and I walk down an open stairway to the first-floor food court. We get coffee and limp croissant sandwiches at a counter and take them to a round table. All around us are people wearing clothes that are almost certainly adorned with plastic buttons from China's Button City.

I ask Peter if he thinks he can keep his button business going.

"Like most manufacturing businesses, we are threatened," he says. "And . . . the government has done nothing at all to support manufacturing in this country. I think it goes back to schools. Children were being told, 'You don't want to go into industry; you might get your hands dirty.' Young people grow up thinking that you can make loads of money just by manipulating financial systems.

"We've got this terrible thing called greed. People only care about making money, and they don't care who they hurt along the way. Everything else goes out the window. I tell my children, 'Leave the country. We're finished.' "

Peter takes a sip of coffee.

"I was brought up [to believe] if you buy something it would last forever. It's a disposable world now," he says. "People buy things and they just expect the stitching won't be good and the buttons will fall off. To me, it's all alien. I just can't live with it.

"Sometimes I think I should have sold the factory and taken the money. I could have, but it would have put people out of work. They rely on me, and I rely on them. I couldn't do it. My father is probably thinking, You stupid idiot—you should have gotten out while you could."

We sit in silence for a few moments. A group of kids in black hooded sweatshirts and ripped skintight jeans walk by.

"But then one day you are walking around the factory and you see a button, and you pick it up, and you say, 'My God, that's a cracking button!' "

Peter's eyes light up with the thought.

"And it drives you on."

CHAPTER 7

The Gold Trimmings

The coat was missing something, John felt. It needed a final flourish, something extraordinary. One day, while he was in the shower, it came to him. His good friend John Thompson was one of the best gold engravers in the world. John wondered if he could commission Thompson to create something special for inside the coat.

The tailor stopped by Thompson's shop in Sydney and told him what he had in mind. Thompson agreed to work up a design that would incorporate the J. H. Cutler logo on one side of a narrow eighteen-karat-gold bar and Keith Lambert's initials on the other. The plaque would be suspended on a gold chain and serve as a hanger inside the collar. He would also carve Keith's initials into a small gold plaque that could be anchored just above the inside breast pocket and take the place of a traditional cloth label. All in all, the two pieces would add about $4,000 to the final price of the coat. The tailor knew that Keith wouldn't mind.

When a work lifts your spirits and inspires bold and noble thoughts in you, do not look for any other standard to judge by: the work is good, the product of a master craftsman.

JEAN DE LA BRUYÈRE

John Thompson works with his thirty-three-year old son, Peter, out of a small, brightly lit studio and salesroom on the fourth floor of the Dymocks Building, an Art Deco landmark in downtown Sydney. The shop is divided by a lighted glass display case holding samples of their work: intricately engraved wedding bands, signet rings, and cufflinks in gold and platinum.

The two sit over microscopes at tables in the back half of their room. The elder Thompson wears a dark denim shirt with the cuffs turned back. He has a broad face, sleepy, kind eyes, white hair, and a trimmed white beard—reminiscent of Ernest Hemingway in his Cuban seafarer period. Peter wears wire-framed glasses and has dark chin stubble and cropped brown hair gelled on top into soft short spikes.

Though it is only 10:30 A.M., John gives off a sense of exasperation that suggests he has already had a long day. Since I arrived and was invited to sit in a chair against the wall, he has misplaced a gold ring, then found it, then misplaced it again, lost to a curiosity shop of desktop clutter: magazines, an old-looking pistol with an engraved handle, tools, crumpled papers, an adding machine, coffee cups, stacks of books, including a battered copy of *Fairbairn's Book of Crests*, a bag of dried apricots, invoices, plastic bags filled with pieces of jewelry and gemstones, and several small metal soldiers, who I assume are strays from the battle-scene diorama set up on a table near me. In the corner, beyond a counter holding a microwave oven and boxes of tea bags, I notice several long-barreled muskets leaning against the wall.

"I like stuff," John says when he sees me scanning the room. "Guns. I get them at auctions. It's bordering on an obsession. This is a ladies' traveling pistol from 1718." He lifts the gun up from his desk to show me.

"Over there, those are Indian muskets, English, Confederate, and Union rifles. It looks like I'm waiting for the next uprisin'," he says, laughing.

John grew up in London's East End and still has the accent and sense of humor of the true Cockney that he is. As a child, he was, of all things, an engraving prodigy. When he was four years old, his father taught him copperplate writing, a style of calligraphy that is transferred by an engraver, using a pointed tool called a burin, onto a plate made of copper. The plate can then be used to make prints. At fifteen, he was accepted into London's Central School of Arts & Crafts, one of the world's most prestigious art institutions, even though the minimum age was eighteen. One school had turned him away because he was already a better engraver than the instructors.

"When I picked up the graver and put it into copper, I knew that this was what I wanted to do," he says.

John happens to be a descendant, on his mother's side, of William Hogarth, the eighteenth-century engraver and painter, whose best-known work is *A Rake's Progress*, a series of images depicting the boozy downfall of a rich young man who comes to the city. "Maybe that's where the obsession comes from."

John's lettering had a balletic flow, and his images were complex, precise, and assured, astonishing in one so young. He was recruited out of art school for a five-year apprenticeship at William Day Limited, a famed copperplate engraver specializing in high-end stationary and naval charts. It would be the last hand-engraving apprenticeship ever offered in the U.K.

"It was quite Dickensian," John says of the firm where he did his training. "My guv'nor had a Sherlock Holmes pipe. I remember one day hearing him completely dismissing offset litho printing, saying it was a 'toy,' that it would never take off. And, really, it pretty much killed off the copperplate industry."

Copperplate engraving produces print images of exquisite sharpness, but because the plates wear down with each strike they have a short life-span. The offset press removed the direct contact between plate and paper by the addition of a rubber surface, allowing for a large number of prints, albeit of lesser quality than copperplate, to be produced rapidly and at a more affordable price. As the use of offset lithography became more widespread, copperplate engraving became increasingly niche.

"The biggest customer in them days was the royal family," John says of his time working in London. "I did the invites for Princess Diana's wedding."

He was also commissioned to craft a gold signet ring with the Welsh three-ostrich-plume crest for Prince Charles's investiture as the Prince of Wales—a ring he still wears on his pinkie.

John moved to Australia in 1983 and, after a short stint in book publishing, started his own jewelry business. He uses engraving methods and tools identical to those used in the fourteenth century, when the craft was first developed to provide ornamentation on suits of armor. With the burin's rounded wooden knob handle resting in the palm of his hand, John pushes the sharp steel tip into precious metal to make a groove, like a plow furrowing a field. The pressure must be exactly right.

"You can always tell an engraver," he says, holding up his right hand and showing me his middle finger, which is permanently twisted from applying force for the past forty-eight years.

Though engraving appears to be a sedentary pursuit, John says it is a physical and mental workout.

"You really use every muscle in your body. And it's also a bit like yoga. You have to control your breathing."

John takes projects home every night, and works on them until 2 A.M. He is usually up by 6 A.M. to make the hour-long commute back into Sydney. Some nights he loses track of time and looks up and realizes that the sun is coming up.

"I always strive for a hundred and ten percent," he says. "I'm never satisfied. That's how passionate I am about it. I eat, drink, and sleep it. I think that's the mark of a true artist. I don't mean to sound conceited."

John's wife is resigned to his long hours. She does not allow him, however, to tell people he is an engraver when they are on vacation, knowing that he will start talking about his work and will be unable to stop.

"She says I have to say I'm a metal worker," he tells me with a laugh.

When John W. Thompson & Son launched several websites, inquiries and orders began coming in. Signet rings were not, it turned out, in demand only among the tallyho set. He is often asked to engrave words in Hebrew, Arabic, and Chinese—none of which he speaks.

"I have got an idea about Latin," he says.

On his left hand, he wears a gold ring on which he carved the words *Cave Furorem Patientis*—"Beware the Fury of a Patient Man."

"There is so much access now. I'm doing five, six, ten jobs at once," he says. "I'm getting overwhelmed. And emails—that's a different kind of hell. People expect me to answer them.

"I'm my own worst enemy, though. I talk too much. I'm always talking to customers who come in. I want them to feel welcome. But I don't like the tire-kickers, the people who want to pick your brain, and then they go home and get on their computers. Or they say, 'Why are you charging so much when I get it done at Mr. Minit?' They don't know how much work is involved."

I think about my own recent brushes with metal engraving: an iPod with my initials on it, and dozens of small personalized trophies for my daughter's ski team. Both purchases had arrived at my front door with stupefying speed after I ordered them online.

John is so skilled with the burin that he can carve sixty letters on a ring measuring only one centimeter across. Just for fun, he once engraved a tiny copper plate with the words "Wishing you a Merry Christmas and Happy New Year," then used it to print his holiday greeting cards. Though John may not be competitive—"I've got past all that. I don't feel I have to prove myself"—hand engravers do have a long tradition of trying to top one another.

The challenge has always been to fit the most words on the smallest surface. In the late 1800s, that might have meant carving the Lord's Prayer on the back of a dollar gold piece. In 1899, a Canadian goldsmith named Samuel Dibbs gained notoriety when he engraved that prayer, plus the Ten Commandments, his name and address, and the words "There are 1,593 letters engraved on this coin" on a five-cent piece. Two years later, the Lord Provost of Perth managed to get the Ten Commandments, the Beatitudes, the Lord's Prayer, Numbers 6:24–26, and the Doxology on a three-penny piece. In 1904, Clarence Young, a U.S. government engraver, fit two full alphabets, the date, and his name on the head of a pin. Then, in 1907, Paul Wentz, a Pennsylvanian, squeezed the Lord's Prayer onto the head of a brass pin with a 2-mm diameter.

That inspired a Seattle jewelry engraver named Godfrey Lundberg to attempt to go one better. His goal was to fit the Lord's Prayer on a pinhead one-third the size of Wentz's. Before he could begin, however, Lundberg knew that he had to undergo serious physical and mental training.

"The steadiness of nerve that would be required could come only as the result of a conditioning process stricter than that of the highly trained athlete," the Spokane *Spokesman-Review* reported. "Tobacco, coffee and like indulgences were out of the question. Fresh air and exercise were necessary. Complete rest for the eyes had to be assured."

As he prepared himself physically, Lundberg also spent six months making an engraving tool of specially tempered steel that could carve microscopic lines but still hold up to the pressure of the engraver's strokes. The point was invisible to the naked eye. Once he had the tool—and the resting heart rate—he worked on the pin only in the evenings, when the rumbling trolley cars that passed by his shop had stopped running for the day. With his arms strapped to an iron bar and his wrists bound with leather straps to muffle the rhythm of his pulse, he completed only two or three strokes a day. After starting over hundreds of times, he finally completed one perfect pin. It had taken him three years—and what was calculated to be 1,863 individual strokes.

The work created a sensation when it went on exhibit at the 1915 Panama-Pacific Exposition in San Francisco. People lined up to pay twenty-five cents for the chance to peer through a microscope at the pin. When that closed, the Lundberg Pin toured the country for two years. Lundberg, meanwhile, had no time to bask in the glory of his feat. He had a nervous breakdown shortly after completing the pin.

"He did recover after about six months of total rest," Jim Austin, his great-grandnephew, told me in an email. The Lundberg Pin, Jim says, is in a safety-deposit box near Seattle.

Nearly a hundred years after Godfrey Lundberg completed his pin, a Birmingham, England, engraver named Graham Short got interested in taking up the Lord's Prayer challenge. The engraver, who was also a champion swimmer with a resting pulse of thirty, wore a stethoscope, and stroked the nineteenth-century needle he was using as a burin only between heartbeats. After successfully completing the pin, he went on to two other unparalleled feats. He fit a chapter from the Koran, in Arabic, on the head of a pin, and the phrase "Nothing Is Impossible" on the barely-there cutting edge of a razor blade.

Becoming accomplished at the most basic hand engraving can take years. More complicated and intricate designs take decades to master. Peter Thompson has been working with his father for thirteen years and still sticks primarily to engraving wedding bands.

"When I started, it took me five days to do one," Peter tells me. "Now I've got it down to maybe five to eight hours. I'm still not up to signet rings."

By the time Peter takes over the business from his father, which he plans to do, he expects to have signet rings in his repertoire as well. Eventually, a third generation may also join the family trade.

"I have a grandson who is sixteen and he's interested in working here," John says. "But I told him, 'Don't just do it because you know you could have a job.' If you haven't got the commitment or the passion for it, it will honestly break your heart."

CHAPTER 8

The Tailor

The canvases, which would create inner structure, had been soaked in water, hung to dry, and then pressed smooth. The same had been done to the pocketing fabric and cotton elements. John had used plenty of steam. It was crucial to get any shrinkage out at the beginning of the process. Now it was time for the making. Here the tailor handed off the work to his two trusted lieutenants in the workroom, Genaro Scura and Leng Ngo.

Leng would handle the interior work: three layers of woolen canvas, horsehair, and cotton would be held together with tiny stitches, laid out in a herringbone pattern. These touches, found "under the hood" of a garment if one knew where to look, are the hallmarks of true bespoke. Mass-produced coats and jackets have glued canvases that can come apart at the dry cleaners—and tend to give the garment a flat appearance. J. H. Cutler garments are three-dimensional: sculptures rendered in cloth.

When the coat was ready for a first fitting, John called Keith and asked him to come by. John and Genaro looked on as Keith slipped the coat on over his suit jacket and turned around to look in the mirror. It was always special, that first moment the client saw himself in the new garment—the dream, Cutler liked to say, made real.

Keith loved the coat. Now it was a matter of getting the details right. They all agreed that it was a little long, so John took one and a half inches off the length. That would make it more pleasing to the eye, and also make it a bit more casual. He also decided to reduce the overlap on the front edge by half an inch. The coat was slightly more voluminous than Keith wanted it to be. No worries, John had told Keith. He would reduce the fullness at the hips.

After the fitting was done, Keith lingered in the shop. John's clients often did. He knew they liked the way they felt there. Safe, special, satisfied. Why not have a spot of something, eh? It was time for a little celebration.

A smack of all Human Life lies in the Tailor; its wild struggles towards beauty, dignity, freedom, victory.

THOMAS CARLYLE

In a paneled private dining room above the dark cabbage palms and gum trees of Sydney's Royal Botanic Gardens, I am fighting the urge to say, "Boxers or briefs?" A silver-haired doctor with a patrician James Mason-y voice and a knack for speaking in long, grammatically gymnastic sentences has just told me that he wears cashmere underwear.

"Bespoke," he adds, with a slight tip of his head, as if that point was very nearly moot. "Of course, it has to have a percentage of nylon to be effective."

"Hmm," I say, nodding and reaching for my champagne glass.

John Cutler is hosting a dinner party for nine friends, all of whom also happen to be longtime customers of his tailoring business. He has dressed for the occasion in a grape-soda-hued mohair-and-wool suit edged with clementine-orange stitching—the color of which just matches the single-breasted jacket's silk lining. His necktie, a shimmery amethyst exclamation point, is nubbed, mid-chest, by a pearl stickpin and set off by a pressed white shirt. Along the top edge of his jacket's breast pocket, a folded handkerchief appears as a flat half-inch bar of white. On his feet are narrow lace-up shoes of black calf and purple suede, custom-made by his friend Stefano Bemer in Florence.

We are on the second floor of the Australian Club, Sydney's oldest and most exclusive gentlemen's retreat. Membership is by invitation only, and must be supported by no fewer than eight current members. That John was nominated and accepted ten years ago is a testament to his genial personality, his personal connections, and the elevation of his profession in the eyes of the city's élite from lowly tradesman to esteemed artisan.

"I've even been asked to be on the wine committee," he told me later. "My forebears would be very surprised."

Women may socialize here in the company of a member, but they are not allowed to join the club. (They are also required to take the elevator to the upper floors—a fact that was pointed out with obvious alarm by the lobby attendant, who halted me as I started up the stairs.) John's guests have moved from the outer lounge area, where cocktails were served, to a long table set with place cards, white linen, silver candelabras, and heavy cutlery. Most of the men appear to be in their sixties. Some are paunchy, some slim; all are freshly shaved and all are wearing dark suits made for them by John Cutler. The discussion, as we were being seated, had been about champagne—and the relative merits of non-vintage versus vintage (my vote, if I had been asked, would have been yes to both). Now the conversation has turned to their collective passion for bespoke—and their devotion to J. H. Cutler.

"I identified myself long ago as someone for whom the comfort zone was essential to maintain," says Philip Knowles, the cashmere-undie-wearing general practitioner seated next to me. "I was greatly threatened by anything that threatened my sense of personal comfort, right down to on my skin. What John excels in is realizing a dream of remarkable personal comfort which is exquisite in its detail, quality, and refinement—and is something about which only you know."

"And, once you are hooked, you are hooked for life," says David Skillman, a trim marketing executive in a red silk tie, seated across from me. "In my case, strange as it may seem, when I first went to work I was amazingly shy. I used to walk by John's father's shop on Bligh Street and look in the window. One day in 1969, I actually walked in. John and I hit it off right away. He made me my first suit—mid-gray mohair and wool. And, after I walked out into the world in my carefully crafted coat of armor, I was invincible. I was Superman. I felt so confident because I knew I had the absolute best, and I could look any other man in this town dead in the eye and say, 'I'm as good as you.' "

"Absolutely." "Quite right," the men huff.

"It's about knowing that you look the best person on the street, that you are wearing something that no one else is wearing, that no one else understands—and you're it," says Tony Wain, a Melbourne-based fabric supplier and the sales agent for Stefano Ricci. "I picked up three pairs of trousers from John today, and I know that when I wear those I'm going to feel absolutely fantastic. It's just so good to know you have something new and something special that is going to fit you and look good and make you feel well."

"That's exactly right—and that shouldn't be underestimated," Philip says, "because the sense of negativity in which you can engage every day, whether as a small businessman or a medical practitioner, is such that it can overwhelm you gradually from one year to the next, let alone one day to the next.

"Yesterday, for example, I had a nineteen-year-old boy stab

his girlfriend in the waiting room. And another person had a heart attack in the waiting room, and yet a third fractured her femur whilst coming up the stairs to the waiting room. These sorts of things happen about once every eight or nine working days. To survive the traumas of practicing medicine, I rely on many arrows in my quiver, and one of the most important arrow for me is this sense of personal comfort . . . and knowing I have around me this little cocoon of Cutlerian elegance and comfort. It allows me to distance myself."

"I can relate so much," says Craig Dyer, the youngest man in the group. Craig is a fit-looking, hyper-groomed forty-something radiologist and champagne bar owner who resembles a less intense Anthony Perkins. "To be able to express yourself and immerse yourself in the joy of [wearing bespoke clothes] . . . it's like art. Going into John's shop is like going into an art gallery. You feel enlightened and enlivened. It helps all the misery you experience during the day go away. It's a bit like my *penchant* for champagne. If I didn't have a little ray of sunshine at the end of the day, there would be no point in me working—no point in me living—because the stress we undergo is enormous."

"Yes." "So true."

"All of my jackets and trousers are John's," Craig continues. "I threw everything else away because they didn't fit right. And I have to say that every time—every single time—I walk out the door, someone comes up to me and says, 'You look very good.' Just tonight, I was waiting for a taxi, and a woman said, 'Love your jacket and trousers,' and just kept walking. When I was in Paris, three complete strangers in the space of a few hours came up to me and said, 'That suit you're wearing is fantastic.' It almost gets embarrassing."

"What about the count, Craig?" John says from the head of the table.

"Ah, the count. The very first garment I got John to make for me was a dinner suit, because I was going to a very official ceremony in France. I had to go up to the front. The Comte Audoin de Dampierre was in the ceremony—he's a very famous count in Champagne. And afterward I was seated and he came over and leaned down and said, 'You are the only person here who is dressed correctly.' And I said, 'But everyone is wearing a dinner suit.' And he said, 'Yes, but yours is the only one that is handmade.' I said, 'How did you know that?' And he said, 'I can tell.' "

"You *can* tell," David Skillman says. "Walking around town, you see what people have on and you look at the buttons and the fit and the cut. It's a certain style and look. You recognize it—and you think, I know what you paid for that, you bastard."

There are chuckles from around the table as the waiters remove the champagne flutes and begin pouring a French Sancerre to accompany small plates of salmon blinis. Someone asks where one buys one's pure cashmere socks—Turnbull & Asser in London, of course—and, yes, they do stock them in cardinal red. Another laments the difficulty of locating anyone who still knows how to darn. A question is raised about the appropriateness of monogrammed buttons.

"I actually think it is a nice touch."

"No, no, never."

"I only do it around the edge," Philip says, pointing to his delicate white pearl shirt buttons.

Phrases I have never heard before are tossed out—"three-quarter hose," "Corby trouser press," "double-cashmere dressing gown." Then there are mystifying declarations, like "One of the greatest disappointments in life is a silk shirt," which carry with them the resonant weight of an epitaph. The waiters present plates of beef tenderloin and fondant potatoes as the men swirl a just-poured New South Wales Shiraz in tulip-shaped glasses and begin to reminisce about Robert Hawke, one of Australia's more dapper past prime ministers.

"He went from dressing in the most dreadful clothes to being superbly dressed. . . . It happened quite suddenly after someone took him to this man," says Michael Egan, the former treasurer of New South Wales, gesturing toward John. "Of course, he had no personal taste. He had to be looked after."

"The first time I met him I was summoned to a meeting," the tailor says. "And I remember walking in and he looked at me rather nervously and said, 'What is this going to do for my polls?' And I said, 'It will be very good for your polls.' And he said, 'All right, let's get on with it, then.' I ended up making him about fourteen suits."

"No one ever noticed his clothes—but that's very often a sign of being well-dressed; people don't actually notice what you are wearing," Michael says.

The discussion then gets a touch heated. The conversation has turned to dry cleaning.

"It's the immersion in fluid which bothers me," Craig says.

"That's why you get suits steam-cleaned," David says.

"It's not the cleaning, it's the pressing afterwards that is the real problem."

"It's got to be blown from below and pressed from above," says Tony. "It takes a long time."

"Just spot-clean."

"Air them."

"All they need is a good brushing. . . ."

"We are willing to pay. We just want it done properly."

"It's a major, major issue," one of the men says with exaggeration, and the others laugh, knowing how they sound.

"I just hand mine to John," Philip says to me.

It would be pleasant, on this late-winter night with a waxing gibbous moon on the rise over Sydney Harbor, in a room full of polite, dignified men who love good suits and loathe shopping and are baffled by the appeal of status brand names—don't get them started on Armani—to think that the dearth of skilled dry cleaners is the thorniest issue of the day. But by the time the roasted rhubarb tart and the selection of cheeses have been served, the mood has shifted.

The men are contemplating the future, a future that must look to them like some dimly lit glass-shelved hell pulsating with house music, where there are no Baccarat snifters of digestifs proffered while one peruses swatches of English wool; no third fittings for cashmere dinner jackets to be worn at the embassy affair; no collegial gatherings, like this one, of like-minded men who understand the ineffable pleasure and the incontestable sagacity of spending $7,000 or more on a well-fitting perfectly executed bespoke suit that will carry them, with perhaps an alteration or two, through the next ten, twenty, even thirty years. They are contemplating a future without J. H. Cutler.

John Cutler's 128-year-old business is struggling. He has been battered by the recession and by made-to-measure start-ups and cheap imports, and certainly by the discouraging lack of good taste and respect for quality that has swept most of society—even among people with plenty of cash. Add to all that the natural attrition of his workforce—in the past four years, he has lost three of his jacket makers, two to cancer and one to retirement—and the resulting drop in production capability, and, well, the picture is not good. He had to completely reorganize his operation in order to make it more economically viable.

On the advice of friends with more business acumen than he, some of whom are in the dining room tonight, he cut overhead and stopped taking a salary. Several of his longtime clients offered to order garments they didn't really need, just to ensure his well-being in the short term. But that doesn't make it any easier to think about what will happen in the next few years. John's two sons, both in their thirties, have zero interest in making clothes. John Handel Lawson Cutler, it is quite clear now, will be the last to pick up the family shears. And it is only a matter of time before he drafts the pattern for his last suit and cuts his final overcoat.

"It's not just John," says Tony, the fabric dealer. "When I started supplying tailors in Victoria, in 1979, I had seventy-three clients. Now I've got five."

"It's a dying art," David says.

"There just aren't any more artisans. . . ."

"But the client base is out there," says one of the men. "It's about marketing . . . tapping into the desire."

"Marketing isn't the issue."

"You have to tap into the psyches of people like us, who appreciate value. John has to get his name out there."

"He's done that."

"It's not marketing."

"There aren't any young people coming into the trade. That's the problem."

"Where would a young person find an apprenticeship today?"

"They can't," Tony says. "They might take a fashion course or a design course. Those are the options. But then they come out and think they are designers—and they're not. They haven't even started. Tailoring starts at age fourteen or fifteen and then, ten years or fifteen years down the track, you may be able to make something. Today, people don't want to work for fifteen years before they make money."

"I don't know what happened to the old European trade idea, but it's gone," David says. "And if we don't get it back we, as a culture, will be the poorer for it."

"People still desire quality, but they have forgotten what it is. They buy things that are expensive and they think they are getting something good, but they're not."

"It's rubbish. . . ."

"Or they spend a lot on a lot of items of clothing and it is all absolute crap."

"It's disposable," says John. "All disposable now."

"That trend is totally contrary to John's having a sustainable business into the future."

"Realistically," Tony says, speaking slowly now, "there is no hope in ten years' time that there will be any tailors left in Australia."

The room falls quiet for a moment.

"What do you do if you want a nice suit?" someone asks.

"You're in trouble."

The Cutler tailoring legacy can be traced back to Australia's mid-nineteenth-century gold-rush days. Huge strikes brought throngs of fortune seekers from Europe, Asia, and America. Among them was John Cutler's great-great-grandfather Joseph Handel Cutler, who traveled by clipper ship in December 1861 from the English Midlands to Melbourne with his wife, a talented dressmaker, and his two young sons. An engineer by trade, he quickly found work in the boomtown of Ballarat.

When Joseph Cutler's oldest son, also named Joseph Handel Cutler, reached his teens, he decided that he wanted to be a tailor, inspired, perhaps, by his mother's sewing skills. He climbed into a red Cobb & Company stagecoach for the long, rattling ride across the bush roads to Sydney, where he found a position as a tailor's apprentice.

Sydney, by then, was thriving. Gas lamps lit the city streets; trams, trains, and ferries had made the growing suburbs accessible. Telephones had been installed. The Bligh Street Turkish Baths had opened, as had the Sydney Lawn Tennis Club, the Royal Sydney Yacht Squadron, the North Sydney Cricket Club, and several men-only social houses, including the Australian Club, patterned after upper-crust London institutions like Boodle's and White's. Bushland ranchers had built elegant homes to be used when they came to town. In the harbor, ships waited to be loaded with wool, tallow, and gold dust. The city was full of people—many of whom had arrived in chains or had parents or grandparents who had arrived in chains—who were suddenly, and against all odds, very rich.

And though this was egalitarian Australia—the land of the "mate"—the haves were not immune to the urge to distinguish themselves from the have-nots. At first, that meant adopting the classic Englishman-in-the-tropics style: white suits, silk shirts, and straw boater hats, according to Margaret Maynard, the author of *Fashioned from Penury: Dress as Cultural Practice in Colonial Australia*.

"Eventually, though, the pressure for conformity to the norms of Europe and the need to demonstrate the maturity and the respectability of colonial society, drove the male bourgeoisie of Melbourne and Sydney into top hats and frock coats," wrote Robert Ross in *Clothing: A Global History*. The fact that the attire was completely wrong for the climate didn't seem to bother them.

"They wear shiny frock-coats and the worst brushed and most odd-shaped of top-hats, and imagine they are well-dressed," sniffed Richard Ernest Nowell Twopenny, an ex-pat English journalist, in his book *Town Life in Australia*. "Can you imagine yourself wearing a black coat and high hat with the thermometer jogging about from 70° to 110° in the shade? If the coat were decently cut, and of good cloth and well-brushed . . . I might put you down a fool, but would admit your claims to be a dandy. But as it is, most of our city men are both uncomfortable and untidy. Their clothes look as if they had been bought ready-made at a slop-shop."

Clearly, there was a need for skilled tailors. In 1884, at the age of twenty-seven, Joseph Cutler opened his own shop, J. H. Cutler, on King Street. By the early 1900s, the firm's customer list was a who's who of Australia's élite. Joseph's son Leslie took over in 1932, and moved the business to larger quarters, occupying four floors in a grand red-brick terraced house at 7 Bligh Street. They would be there for the next fifty years, eventually employing nearly two dozen tailors on two floors of workrooms.

Leslie Cutler was a stickler. One morning, looking out the window of the shop, he saw a man wearing a suit he had delivered just the day before walking into the Union Club across the street. The man, he noticed with alarm, was wearing the wrong shoes for the suit. He called the club and had the customer summoned to the telephone.

"Sir," he said, "I made that suit to be worn with black shoes, not brown."

Cutler suits did not come cheap. "I was always given a chair while [Cutler] made out a receipt," recalled the 1930s memoirist Lydia Gill, who was sometimes sent to pick up garments for her boss. "The suits being paid for were usually about 25 pounds each—a house could be furnished for about 50 pounds. I was staggered, and really needed that chair so graciously produced."

In 1939, Leslie's son Bruce returned from London, where he had spent a few years studying the trade, to manage the family business. Thirty years later, Bruce's son, John Handel Lawson Cutler—with whom I am now riding in a silver Jaguar borrowed from his client Craig Dyer, through the streets of Sydney's leafy northern suburbs—would follow the same path to the by then legendary shop on Bligh Street.

"I never wanted to do anything else," John says. We are driving into Wahroonga, down streets shaded by broad fig trees and past grandly restored Arts and Crafts–style houses set behind trimmed Viburnum hedges. John is wearing what for him must be the obvious choice for a morning drive: a lightweight suede bomber jacket, pleated navy cotton-and-cashmere corduroy trousers, a checked shirt, and a sky-blue silk knit necktie. "Drake's of London," he says of the tie when I ask. His handmade Italian shoes—"Stefano Bemer"—exactly match his jacket's caramel hue.

"I was sewing under the table at school. I made waistcoats for the teachers," he tells me.

John grew up nearby, in the suburb of Pymble. At sixteen, the same year he saw the Beatles play in concert at Sydney Stadium, he graduated from Sydney Grammar, a well-regarded private school, and began working in the workroom in the mornings. In the evenings, he learned the basics of sewing, cutting, and making patterns. In 1966, at the age of eighteen, he sold his drum kit and his Honda motor scooter to buy a ticket for England on board the fourteen-hundred-passenger *Castel Felice*, a gleaming white Italian liner.

"I had two brand-new suits that the firm had made for me. My other prized possession was an oversized pillar-box-red, roll-necked jumper that my sisters knit to keep me warm in the English winter. It became very much a talking point on the ship."

There was plenty of time to admire John's oversized sweater: the voyage lasted five and a half weeks.

"It became like our own country," he says.

John drank Bacardi and Cokes and danced to the four-piece band, whose members, in shiny red jackets and black bow ties, played Beatles tunes again and again as the ship steamed east. There were folk-singing lessons and card games in the Verandah Lounge, pillow fights on beams above the swimming pool, and a traditional Crossing the Equator "baptism" ceremony during which plates of spaghetti were dumped on the heads of passengers who had been plucked out of the crowd.

"The first time I ever saw snow was when we arrived in Southampton on December eighth. I remember waking up and looking out at the wharves covered in white. I checked into a hotel near the Marble Arch in London. The morning after I arrived, I rushed out of the hotel and slipped on the ice on the top step and ended up on my rear end in the street."

John went to the Tailor and Cutter Academy in London's West End, which, from the time it was established in 1866 until it shut its door in the 1970s, was the Oxford University of tailoring.

"I used to drive around on a motorcycle—this skinny kid in a huge red sweater riding a Royal Enfield 750cc. It was the height of swinging London—Carnaby Street, music, fashion. And then there were the bowler-hatted clients on Savile Row. I loved the contrast of it all."

John wandered the food hall in Fortnum & Mason, drank Newcastle Brown Ale in the Glassblower pub, sipped tea at the Ritz, admired the miniskirted women coming out of Mary Quant, and got a job at Dormeuil, the Paris fabric merchant, whose London headquarters was in an imposing six-story Edwardian building in Golden Square, close to Savile Row.

"My first job there was making pattern books. I got to know all about different fabrics. Then I was moved to the Home Trade department. I remember handling vicuña back then. If you were a salesperson who needed samples, you had to get a director of the firm to come and unlock the cages where the vicuña was kept. It was in sixty-meter rolls—in navy, black, and natural. There was a lot of talk about an Arab sheikh who used it for curtains for his palace; it was all done with suitcases full of cash."

John came back to Sydney in 1969, before his twenty-first birthday, with a diploma in "cutting gentlemen's tailor-made garments." He had also adopted a personal style that turned heads.

"Shortly after I returned, walking down the platform of a city train station wearing spats and a homburg hat and carrying a walking stick, I ran into one of my best friends," John continues. "He was dumbfounded. He and his fiancée had been staring and laughing at me, before they realized it was me. And I got beaten up once by a bunch of bikies in leather jackets. I was coming home from work in a rather smart suit, cane, and hat. I was a choice target."

John, I am learning, comes by his quirkiness honestly. His family tree is filled with exotic fruit: red-haired operetta singers who lived in arctic log cabins; London massage-parlor owners; bareback riders who raced with Indians in the wilds of Calgary; heavy drinkers of whiskey who eschewed doctors and lived into their hundreds. His father, a champion rugby player, met his mother playing leapfrog in Kew Gardens. John himself has been married four times and has three grown children and a thirteen-year-old daughter, whose mother is a former live-in girlfriend. A few months prior to my arrival in Sydney, his wife of two years had left him while he was in London on a business trip. He came home and she was gone. No note, no nothing.

"The financial pressures," he says, "were perhaps too much to bear." And, he is, he's afraid, something of a flirt.

We are headed for an early lunch at the home of Karl Sussmann, John's friend, client, and former business associate. Karl, John has told me, is the grandson of Bertie Oldfield, the legendary Australian cricket player, who was as famous for his fastidious dress as he was for having his skull fractured in 1932 by a vicious "body line bowl"; the incident was the source, for a time, of a diplomatic chill between Australia's and England's cricket federations.

"When Karl turned twenty-one, Bertie asked me to make him a suit and to take him under my wing, to be a kind of style mentor for him," John says, as he turns down a narrow driveway to a brick cottage with a peaked red-tile roof and a white-railed front porch. In the front yard, workers are laying a pathway. "Karl ended up joining the company, learned to cut trousers, and served as the company's business manager."

When Karl came into some money, he left the business. Since then, he has been a loyal client.

"I've made dozens of things for him over the years—suits,

overcoats, shirts, jackets, trousers," John says. "He also has an incredible shoe collection—custom, from all the world-class makers. He polishes them every day."

Karl Sussmann is a lean man in pressed tan pants and a navy cashmere V-neck, who radiates a yogi's quiet intensity. Though he is welcoming, I sense that he is also someone who would not appreciate being interrupted while he is trimming the perfectly spherical potted topiary trees that border one side of the swimming pool in his landscaped rectangular back yard. His house, done in dove grays, gives off the same disciplined serenity. When lunch is served, we sit at a dining table that has been set with goblets, silver, large exotic-looking blooms, and gray damask linens. There is a chilled bottle of 2008 Savaterre Chardonnay on the table. It is eleven-forty in the morning.

I say something like "Nice napkins."

"Aren't they wonderful? They are so capacious. Great for tucking in," he says. "They are from a Paris flea market. I bought them all."

Over lunch, Karl gives me his carefully considered theories about clothing and style and *sprezzatura*—a kind of nonchalant dash perfected by Italians.

"There is a progression of sartorial knowledge," he says. "Maybe you start with Corneliani or Brioni, then made-to-measure, then up the ramp to bespoke.

"Bespoke is as far away from fashion as you can get. I almost think of it as anti-consumerism. I don't consume. Everything I purchase now is a keeper."

After lunch, Karl walks us back past the topiaries and out to the front yard. The air is scented with the blue-green bite of eucalyptus. The bricklayers are still at work. We stand in the sun, looking at their progress.

"I am a particular person. I'm not trying to be difficult. But I do have Rock of Eye," he says, referring to the expression used by tailors to describe the ability to know instinctively when something is right and true. "If you have it, you apply it in every aspect of life. For instance, the other day I looked at the path here, and I said to the workers, 'That's off by a full centimeter.' And they measured it. I was right. It is a bit of a demon. You only see the flaws."

On our way back to the city, John says, "There are six or seven kinds of bespoke customers. There are fanatics like Karl. They know what they want and they know I can make it. They come to me for the technical skills. They want the best quality, and they are very, very particular. They will count the stitches on a collar. I don't know what makes them that way. Karl calls it a sickness. Some people really get addicted to it. They always have to have something new. It's got nothing to do with clothing; it's about not allowing themselves to be satisfied.

"Then there are people who see their tailors as people they can take their frustrations out on. They make totally unreasonable demands. I will do anything for someone who is genuine and passionate, but I have become very tough when I sense people are trying to use me or they are being unreasonable. They want things that are impossible. I mean, fabric is fluid; when you stand in a different position, it is going to look different.

"Other people come for traditional reasons—J. H. Cutler made for their fathers and grandfathers, so when it is time to get a suit, they come to me. Some come for a one-off—a wedding suit, father of the bride, or something for a special meeting, or maybe they have been saving up to get this one thing. I may never see them again.

"Then there are people who are label-conscious and snobby

about it. They act like 'Look out. I'm wearing Cutler.' I have even been asked to sew one of my Cutler labels into a coat on which I am only doing an alteration. They can't afford it, but they want to show off. Of course, there are some people who just can't buy off the rack—dwarves, giants, humpbacks.

"Others come because they need guidance. They haven't a clue. They know they have to dress well because of their station, but they don't really care and they don't want to have anything to do with it. They say, 'Just make me something I can put on,' or 'Make me another one just like the last one.'

"I have a client who has ordered exactly the same garments in the same style and fabrics for the last thirty or forty years— a plain navy, a plain charcoal, a blue pinstripe, a gray pinstripe, a Prince of Wales check, and a dinner suit. When I couldn't find the exact same fabrics, I had to scramble to find acceptable substitutions. A little while back, he got divorced and remarried, and his new wife wanted a say in what he wore. That didn't last long."

We are crossing the Harbour Bridge. Below us, commuter ferries leave frothy wakes in the blue chop as they chug past the stegosaurian roof plates of the Sydney Opera House.

"How would you categorize Keith Lambert?" I ask.

"Keith is someone who regards quality as being really important—the main thing. Those kinds of people don't know much of anything about tailoring, but they can see and feel the quality, and they know it is something they can't find in ready-to-wear. And they want it."

John has some clients who defy categorization, including Boy George, Elton John, and the Greek Orthodox archbishop of New York. Then there was one especially devoted and wealthy client who ordered seventy-five suits in the 1980s, to be made over a period of many years, just to ensure that John Cutler would never have a slack period.

"One thing I really love about this business is that you get to meet and deal with people from all walks of life on a very, very personal basis," John says. "When you get into the fitting room without your trousers on, it's a great leveler."

John operates by appointment only, out of a small carpeted showroom on the sixth floor of an Art Deco building in the city's high-rise financial district. A nineteenth-century cedar cutting table, purchased by his great-grandfather and passed down through four generations of Cutlers, dominates the space. Positioned in front of a long wall that has been curtained with pleated blue-black silk and illuminated by a bank of overhead lights, it looks very much like an altar—a place for followers to pay homage to the great demigod of ticket pockets and rolled lapels. And now, after crossing the room and running my hand over it, I do feel I am in the presence of something just a little sacred. It was on this nicked and burnished tabletop that John cut the vicuña cloth for Keith Lambert's coat.

John wants to get a pattern done for a jacket before the end of the workday. He has taken off his suit coat, draped a tape measure around his neck, and laid out a piece of pattern cardboard on the cutting table. He places his T square and makes a series of pencil marks on the paper, then uses a straight ruler to connect the dots. He makes more marks, draws more lines, working quickly, humming and chatting, consulting his notes, measuring, drawing. With every line, the diagram grows more complex— and less decipherable to a layperson like me—until at last he is satisfied that he has drafted an accurate and detailed map of his client, imperfections noted and accommodated for. John finishes the pattern, and Craig Dyer, the radiologist cum champagne expert, arrives—as he does every Monday—with a bottle.

"I always bring a little something around and have a chat," Craig says.

This evening he has another reason to be here; the jacket he is having made is ready for a fitting. Craig has chosen Dormeuil's Jade, the silky and very expensive British-made navy wool woven in West Yorkshire and tumbled in the finishing process at W. T. Johnson, in Huddersfield, with minute bits of jade stone. He slips on the half-finished jacket, which is tracked vertically with long white baste stitches, and stands motionless with his eyes toward the ceiling while John inspects it. The tailor pinches in a little fabric in the back and at the shoulder, smoothing the lapels, picking a bit of lint off one arm. When he is done, Craig turns to see himself in a three-way mirror.

"John," he says, "it is perfection."

Like all great master tailors, John Cutler is an exacting engineer, an intuitive artist, and a silver-tongued salesman. He is also often a therapist to his clients—encouraging the timid, propping up the dispirited, and soothing the stressed. (Unlike other professionals who are obligated to be discreet, however, he is expected to cultivate client relationships outside the consultation room, which he does with an Aussie's characteristic gusto.)

John's job is to discern what a man looks like most of the time, when he is not in front of the tailor's mirror. He could tell right away if you had stopped going to the gym or had been overindulging in martinis or meat pies. He could sense when your confidence had flagged or your relationships were in turmoil. He could tell when you had a new love or when things were going great guns at work. It was all about carriage. Posture. Confidence.

John never judges. He measures accurately, and without prejudice. And he always makes it clear: there is no point in trying to suck in your stomach.

"Come on, now, no cheating. Relax or I will have to tickle," he would say.

John may be many things, but what he is not is a seamster. Though he has the skills to produce a garment from start to finish, the needle-and-thread stuff—the work most people think of when they hear the word "tailor"—is done by a team of four stitchers in a basement atelier seven floors below John's showroom.

The workshop is a brightly lit windowless room just off the elevator. Rolls of pastel shirting cottons and jewel-toned silks and satins lean in the corners; folds of dark suitings are stacked on shelves. On the worktables, there are scraps of cloth, rulers, scissors, chalk, beeswax cakes, display cards of gold blazer buttons, pillow-like pressing hams, and heavy flatirons. Blazers, trousers, and tuxedo jackets, in various stages of completion, hang on racks and off pegs.

Genaro Scura, bald and bespectacled, with one eyebrow arched inquisitively higher than the other, occupies the area closest to the door. He is wearing dark trousers, a blue-and-white striped shirt, and a necktie. On the wall above his worktable, he has taped photos of Princess Diana, Kate Middleton, the Sydney Opera House, Mary MacKillop—Australia's first canonized saint—and Keith Lambert's vicuña coat. At sixty-six, Genaro is the senior member of the team. He is also the group's designated jacket maker, the title reserved for the most skilled tailors. Jackets and coats are complex, painstakingly shaped and padded garments that require a sculptor's eye and a surgeon's hand. The stitching alone in a suit jacket takes about forty-eight hours; trousers, by contrast, with their simple long seams, can be finished in ten to twelve hours.

Genaro stands up to say hello. He has a pronounced curvature of the upper spine—the "tailor's hump" that is common among men who have spent most of their lives bent over sewing projects. (The craft has lent its name to other maladies: "tailor's bunions"—a painful swelling on the fifth metatarsal brought on by the crossed-legged "tailor's pose" sitting position many once assumed in order to get their work closer to their eyes—and the far more dire "tailor's disease," another name for tuberculosis, which swept through sweatshops in the late 1800s.)

The son of a shoemaker, Genaro was born in 1945, in Cosenza, a small village in Calabria, Italy. When it was time to select a trade, his father steered him into tailoring. At ten, Genaro learned how to stitch; at twelve, he went to work full-time for a local tailor. In 1963, at the age of eighteen, he left home and headed to Rome to get experience with one of the best tailors in Italy. It was the height of Hollywood's obsession with *la dolce vita*. Genaro remembers George Hamilton coming in for fittings.

"I make for him suits, in the blue mohair and the beige gabardine. I still remember," he says. "Very handsome, very young."

In 1969, Genaro moved to Australia and started looking for work.

"I saw an ad in the paper for a job with Giuseppe Simonella," Genaro says. Simonella was an accomplished Italian tailor who had trained at Brioni before moving to Sydney to start his own business. Genaro joined Simonella, and stayed for twenty-five years.

"That's why I don't speak so much English. I don't have to."

Genaro joined J. H. Cutler in 1995. Now he is just a year or two away from retiring—and from leaving a gaping hole in John's workroom. Though the tailoring team includes a young assistant, a talented Daniel Radcliffe look-alike named Rhys Twist, who seems committed to learning the trade, they have found that, in general, interns and apprentices move on after a few months.

"The new generation, they don't like to take the time to learn anymore this job," Genaro says. "Too hard, very hard. They need too much time, too much patience."

"For the money, they would rather go and drive a bus," John says. "It takes years and years and years of work. The old apprenticeships in England were five years, but when you are finished, really, you were just starting to learn. Five years was just for the technical bits. Genaro will tell you, you learn every day. Every cloth is different, every figure is different. Rhys will learn certain things, but he won't learn the real thing. He needs someone like Genaro to teach him. And Genaro will be gone."

John often brings Genaro up to the showroom to be in on fitting sessions. Some favored customers even get to go downstairs to watch the tailors at work.

"I like to do that with the ones who are nice people," John says. "I don't introduce the hard ones."

Sometimes the customers don't want to leave.

"We had a young Chinese man from Perth come in," John recalls. "He was on holiday and we had corresponded by email before he arrived, sorting out what he wanted. When he got here, I cut the pattern and the cloth, and he stood and watched me do everything. Then he went down and sat in the workroom for ten days. He watched every stitch. He was at the door when we opened and he went to lunch with the guys. He had come to Sydney to see his suit being made. It was his first one."

I ask Genaro if he minded being watched like that.

"It's okay for me. I feel secure in what I am doing."

Genaro was excited when John came to him with the idea of making Keith Lambert's vicuña overcoat entirely by hand.

"I want to see how they do before machines," he says. "And I prefer working with difficult materials. Everyone can do easy. I want to know what I can do."

Genaro worked on the coat for two solid weeks, putting the needle in and drawing it out, advancing the seams stitch by stitch, inch by inch. At the same time, his colleague Leng Ngo, who is J. H. Cutler's foreman, was crafting the coat's innards—the padding and linings that would give it shape.

Leng, who has joined us at the table, is a slender boyish-looking forty-two-year-old Cambodian who escaped to Vietnam from Phnom Penh in 1975, when he was six years old.

"We left the capital city and suddenly it is very difficult—nothing to eat, nothing to drink, nowhere to live," he tells me. "Trucks would run over the bodies sleeping in the street. They didn't care. The river had bodies in it, but you had to drink. You remember those things."

With the financial help of two brothers who were living in Australia, he enrolled in tailoring school in Saigon. When he was eighteen, he and his family were able to join them in Sydney. A school counselor helped Leng get a week's worth of experience in J. H. Cutler's workroom.

"I was impressed with his attitude," John says. When Leng was done with school, John hired him full-time.

"As team leader, I have to be quick-thinking," Leng says of his role in the workshop. "I say to the team, 'Nothing is impossible. Let's work together; let's make it happen. We will support each other.'"

Teamwork is especially needed when clients request rush jobs.

"We had a retired Russian atomic-sub captain come into the shop once," John says. "He was only going to be in Sydney for a few days. He didn't speak any English; he arrived with an inter-preter, a very pretty girl. He wanted the best—and he didn't want anything Italian. He said there were too many Italian suits in Moscow. So we had to get the cloth flown over from Scabal; it was a Super 250. Money was never mentioned. It was a nineteen-thousand-dollar suit. He was very pleased."

"People are so happy. They say, 'How you do that?'" Leng says. "I really enjoy it. Every day I feel excited. To stay and work twenty-two years, I must be feeling love."

"Leng told me once that when he came to work for me it was the day he was born," John says.

After nearly a week in Sydney, I have given up trying to guess what would be appropriate to wear on an outing with John Cut-ler. He has his own internal dress code—one that never, ever includes "casual." For a sightseeing flight on a harbor seaplane, he wore a suit coat of black wool flecked with random pea-size white dots, white wool trousers, a black beret, and black suede tasseled shoes. Craig Dyer, who had come along on the trip, was in a tan silk-and-cashmere suit with a white dress shirt and no necktie.

"You told me to dress down," he had said to John as we sat on an open skiff, getting splashed with Sydney Harbor water on our way out to where the seaplane was moored.

For a ferry trip to Manly, a surf resort town six miles north of the city, John donned a light-purple cashmere-and-silk jacket with a white pocket square, black wool trousers, and a white-and-purple striped shirt, the cuffs of which were held together by gold cufflinks engraved by John Thompson. His friend, the writer and historian Bruce Stannard, who was joining us, had been easy to spot at the dock. He was wearing a Cutler-made three-piece Harris Tweed suit, with a dark-blue shirt and a moss-colored knit tie and substantial saddle-brown brogues. He looked dressed for a moorland ramble, or something involving grouse.

In Manly, under a low overcast sky, we had walked along the sickle-shaped beach and the choppy Tasman Sea, past overweight young mothers in straining sweatpants and sulky, narrow-eyed surfer boys in hoodies and baggy board shorts. John and Bruce had followed me into a surf shop and stood near the wetsuits with their hands clasped behind their backs while I hastily picked out T-shirts for my daughters. The kid behind the cash register stared at them as if they were alien beings.

But John Cutler is used to being stared at. In fact, he seems to relish it. On one of my last mornings in Sydney, I meet him at his apartment in Potts Point, on the quarried ridge above Woolloomooloo Bay. The plan is to take a long walk following the contours of the harbor through the Botanic Gardens, past the Opera House, along Circular Quay, and up to Observatory Hill Park, overlooking the water and the muscular arch of Sydney's famous bridge. I notice that most of the people strolling the paved shoreline walkway, or sprawling on picnic blankets or sitting on the sea wall in the milky winter sun, are wearing jeans, T-shirts, and sneakers—myself included. It makes perfect sense: who wouldn't want to be comfortable and have well-cushioned feet? But, as a group, we look unkempt, rumpled, and dull.

John Cutler, on the other hand, is marching along under the hoop pines and giant figs in bright-fuchsia trousers, of a fluttery wool faille, and a dark-pink-and-white checked cotton shirt. He has on matching suede shoes and is carrying a walking stick. Almost everyone we pass looks him up and down. A few people comment on his ensemble.

"Do you enjoy that?" I ask. "Being looked at?"

"It's not that I think I'm good-looking. I'm not good-looking," he says. "But I dress the way I feel. If I'm feeling chirpy, I like to show it with color. And I guess I'm saying, 'You can do this, too.' I want to challenge people's perceptions, get them out of their comfort zone. People say, 'But that's not normal.' I don't care if it's normal or not. I believe in the individual, rather than the masses. The masses are made up of individuals, but they don't realize it. Most of them just fit in."

We walk on, past outdoor cafés and souvenir shops selling boomerangs and Ugg boots. Near the ferry docks, an Aboriginal man, with a painted face and bare feet, is sitting on an overturned plastic crate playing the didgeridoo. The long wooden wind instrument emits a froggy vocalized drone, like an aural toothache. In a while, I get up the courage to ask John how he feels about being the last in the long line of Cutler tailors.

"What makes me sad is not the name Cutler going away," he says. "It's the trade. I can't see that the old skills can be taught sufficiently well for real tailoring to continue.

"But things change. You go back to the days of the dandies or the French courtiers. People wouldn't have a clue in the world now how to do all that. It's the same progression. Maybe one day we'll have spray-on suits. You get up and you go to the bathroom, you do your stuff, and you spray something on you. Virtual suits. I mean, who knows? Who knows. I think it's time. The world changes, and you have to change with it."

CHAPTER 9

The Coat

After the first fitting, the coat was disassembled, pressed, and re-marked. Then John handed it back to Leng and Genaro. He knew they were relishing their freedom. There were no time or cost constraints. The challenge was simply to produce their very best work.

The inside and outside of the pockets were constructed; the silk lining was cut and stitched into place. The facing was attached and the back seam finished. Then it was all put together again for a second fitting. Keith returned, and the coat was marked for slight adjustments and sent back down to the workroom.

There was not much left to do. The side and shoulder seams were finished, the pads were put into place, and the sleeves were made. The collar was hand-shaped using a heavy iron—the goal was a rounded fit without any bubbling. The undercollar and the sleeves were basted into place.

Keith came back for a third fitting, to double-check the balance of the sleeve and to make sure that the height and the fullness in the collar were perfect. To allow for Keith's lower shoulder, John felt that the right sleeve needed to be pitched slightly back.

Back in the workroom, Genaro finished the sleeves and the collar and made the buttonholes. Then he used a beeswaxed four-cord thread to attach the navy buttons. He sewed on the gold plaque and chain, and then gave the whole thing one final press, using a sixteen-pound iron. The overcoat was done.

Keith arrived for the final fitting. John smiled broadly as his client

slipped it on. The fit, the drape, the silhouette, and the workmanship—
all superb. If this was the last garment he ever made, John Cutler
could die happy. Keith invited the tailor to dinner at his waterfront
house in Mosman, on what was known as Millionaire's Mile. When
John arrived, Keith had a bottle of champagne for him, brought up
from the wine cellar—something extra-special.

Costly thy habit as thy purse can buy,
But not express'd in fancy; rich, not gaudy,
For the apparel oft proclaims the man

WILLIAM SHAKESPEARE

I am in the high-ceilinged lobby of one of Vancouver's swankest hotels, which occupies the first fifteen floors of a skyscraper. Massive crystal chandeliers, which would look a bit much hanging in Versailles, illuminate groupings of square-backed chocolate-brown leather couches and chairs. Black lacquer screens and big-leafed potted plants are strategically placed in corners on the parquet sandstone floor. One wall is dominated by a two-story-high Chinese-character painting, done on rice paper in what looks like the single stroke of an ink-dipped mop.

There is no front desk. Instead, members of the staff escort guests to their suites for a private check-in. I am not checking in, I tell the young man who has glided to me as if wearing small hovercrafts for shoes. I am here to see a resident. He shows me to the elevator that will take me to one of the building's top-floor penthouse apartments. This is where I will find Keith Lambert, who has invited me to visit while John Cutler is also in town. John had flown in from Sydney the day before to deliver some new clothes to his client.

This is where I will find the vicuña overcoat. As the elevator rises, I feel nervous and jangly, as if I were about to meet in the flesh someone with whom I have been carrying on a lengthy and intimate online relationship. I knock on Keith's door, and in a moment he appears and invites me in. Keith, a tall, fit man in a tweed jacket and striped tie, is holding Rosie, the dog, under his arm. He is soft-spoken, very polite, and obviously a little wary about having a writer in his apartment, wanting to see his clothes.

Through the floor-to-ceiling windows is a sweeping view of the city, the harbor, and Vancouver Island. Tiny black-and-red-hulled freighters dot English Bay, blue under a bluer sky. In the apartment, giant ceramic vases sit beneath abstract paintings hung on mocha-colored walls. A glass vase of yellow and lavender tulips is centered on an antique-looking Chinese table. Built-in lacquered shelves hold low stacks of oversized books. I can read some of the titles on the bindings: *Porsche. Fois Gras. Bulgari. Vogue.*

I greet John Cutler, who, in a black jacket, white silk vest, lavender tie, and striped trousers, could be dressed for his own wedding. After a moment or two, John steps to one side and says, with a sweep of his arm, "Here it is."

The vicuña overcoat is draped across the back of a dark-brown rattan sofa. One edge has been turned back to expose the blue-printed silk lining.

"The coat," I say.

I reach for it, saying, "Can I . . . ?" Without waiting for an answer, I stroke the soft nap, touch a button, and then open up the coat to take in the full glory of the lining. I rub a finger lightly across the letters "J. H. Cutler" on the engraved gold plaque.

"It's beautiful."

"Why don't you put it on for her?" John says, and hands the coat to Keith. John buttons it for him, and brushes some lint from one shoulder. I ask Keith to pose for me, which he does sheepishly, grinning, with his arms hanging straight down. I snap the picture.

"Could I try it on?" I ask. Keith takes off the coat and holds it out for me. My arms slip along the liquid lining in the sleeves and the coat settles on my shoulders. I look down at the buttons, slide my hands into the pockets, then pull them out and run them down the coat, feeling the plush.

"Beautiful," I say again. I can't believe I have it on.

"The coat!" I say, wrapping my arms around myself, with the long sleeves flapping.

John and Keith beam.

Before Keith can back his Porsche Cayenne out of his parking space in the underground garage below his building, he has to first spread a small white towel across his lap. Rosie sits here while her owner drives. The towel helps protect Keith's trousers, which are bespoke and made by John Cutler, who is now in the backseat.

We are going to do some shopping before lunch. Keith drives a few blocks to Holt Renfrew, an upscale department store in the heart of the city. We use the valet parking in the basement and take the elevator up to the menswear floor. An obsequious salesman, who seems to recognize Keith, escorts us through the Tom Ford, Zegna, Canali, Armani, Gucci, Loro Piana, and Balmain departments, stopping to discuss fabrics and stitching and silhouettes. Keith looks at a suit or two, and peruses some ties. I trail along, fighting the urge to check price tags. In a while, Keith has had enough and, he says, he wants to get back to the car to make sure Rosie is all right.

"I didn't see anything that interested me," he says, explaining why he's leaving empty-handed.

Over lunch, I ask Keith if he gets compliments when he wears the coat or other Cutler-made clothing.

"No, not really," he says. "I'm not sure any of my friends really get bespoke."

"Do you worry about the coat when you wear it out?" I ask.

"If I can secure it, get a ticket at a coat check, I'll hand it over. If I can't, I'll roll it up on my seat."

The salads are cleared. We drink some wine.

"Tell Meg about the next one," John says to Keith.

"Well, I have a birthday coming up," he says. "And I have always had my eye on a second coat—especially now that I've relocated to Canada. I thought, Why not? I could buy a car, but I would only have the car for a few years."

"Keith has asked me to make him another vicuña overcoat," John says. "In the tan."

EPILOGUE

Those who find beautiful meanings in beautiful things are the cultivated. For these there is hope.

OSCAR WILDE

Keith Lambert did get the tan vicuña coat made, in a style almost identical to the navy. John lined this one with Hermès silk scarves in a bright red, blue, and orange polo-pony print. Among Keith's other notable recent J. H. Cutler commissions are a formal Scottish kilt ensemble finished with solid silver buttons and a dinner jacket in lightweight cream-colored wool. For an upcoming cruise vacation, John had suggested that Keith pair the jacket with matching cream trousers, and accessorize with a handmade Borsalino straw hat and Edward Green mink-suede shoes.

"For a more informal look, it works very well indeed," John said of the outfit.

In mid-2012, the tailor got another call from his loyal client. Keith wanted to make sure John still had that length of black vicuña in the back room—the third and final piece of the vintage Dormeuil cloth. He said that he had been thinking he would like a full-length cape to wear over the kilt or a dinner suit.

For inspiration and guidance, John turned to his grandfather's collection of tailoring books, and there, in one from 1870, he found instructions for the cutting and sewing of a gentleman's cape.

"The author of the book suggested that an ideal fabric for the cape would be vicuña. So I knew it was perfect," John told me on the phone.

Though he had yet to settle on a final design, he thought he would suggest to Keith that it be a reversible garment, one side the black vicuña and the other a vivid cashmere—perhaps red, yellow, or blue.

Meanwhile, in Florence things have been going very well for Stefano Ricci. On a hot June night in 2012, the designer celebrated his company's fortieth anniversary by presenting his 2013 spring and summer collection in the West Hallway of the Uffizi—a first for the museum. Men in handmade slim white suits, black crocodile jackets, and safari-style khakis had stridden past Baccio Bandinelli's muscular *Laocoön* and down the sculpture-lined makeshift runway while guests fanned themselves with programs. The climax of the show was the appearance of eight Masai warriors, draped in red cloth and wielding spears, who did a traditional jumping dance as Stefano and Filippo took their bows. Stefano, who had been made an honorary tribal chief in acknowledgment of his generosity to Masai villages, had flown them in for the show. Later, two hundred invited guests had dined under a new moon on the Uffizi's terrace. Just before midnight, the group walked out to the Loggia dei Lanzi to see the dramatic debut of a computerized lighting system, donated to the city of Florence by Stefano.

The new Stefano Ricci Beverly Hills store opened in 2011, followed by boutiques in Zurich, Vienna, Abu Dhabi, Paris, Ankara, and Doha, among others, bringing the total to twenty-five—with more shops planned. Stefano has also started a new division designing interiors for luxury boats. His first project, a

230-foot mega-yacht to be exhibited at the 2012 Monaco Yacht Show, featured his signature dark hardwood, travertine tile, and orange crocodile-skin upholstery. And, in the fall of 2012, he announced that he would open a new atelier in Florence, where all sewing machines were banned. His only recent disappointment was his failure, on his last African hunting trip, to bag the elusive giant croc.

In London, meanwhile, Savile Row tailors found themselves facing yet another assault from Abercrombie & Fitch. The American retail chain announced that it would be opening an Abercrombie children's store at 3 Savile Row, right next to Gieves & Hawkes. The news spurred a group of well-groomed protesters wearing vintage bespoke suits to take to the street, chanting, "All we are saying is give three-piece a chance."

The cheeky demonstration got wide press coverage—and helped persuade the Westminster Council to rule that the new store would not be allowed to play music that could be heard on the street and could not have customers park baby carriages on the sidewalk—but it did not stop A&F's march on the Row. Many of the tailors were shaken.

As one said, anonymously, to a reporter, "I don't think anyone objects to moving forward, but a chain store selling crappy clothes to ghastly people isn't really the direction in which we should be traveling."

Still, there was some reason for good cheer. *Downton Abbey*, the Emmy Award–winning British costume drama, took the United States by storm. By the end of its second season, in 2012, bespoke tailors and shoemakers said they were seeing a surge in orders from Americans who wanted the classic English country gentleman look.

Meanwhile, Frédéric Dormeuil took a sabbatical from the

family business to enroll in a one-year intensive MBA program to be completed in Shanghai, São Paulo, and San Francisco. Dormeuil headquarters moved to a more modern facility, also in Palaiseau, France. Machines now cut basic fabrics; high-end cloths are still being cut by hand.

In Peru, Jane Wheeler moved CONOPA's administrative operations to a new office, away from the university. The organization is being flooded with new projects.

"There seems to be a respect for CONOPA which [wasn't] there before," she told me in an email.

A two-month-long official census of vicuña was to start in the fall of 2012, the first since 2000. Wheeler said she expected the numbers to be up. Prices for raw, cleaned vicuña fiber were holding steady at about $650 per kilo. (English cloth makers, meanwhile, were paying $1,850 per kilo to their vicuña-fiber suppliers.) Jane has shifted her focus, for the time being, from vicuña to the endangered guanaco, South America's other wild camelid, on a project funded by a mining operation.

In the mills of West Yorkshire, business has slowed down.

"We have had a good run—busy for nearly three years," Bryan Dolley told me when I checked in. "We have seen it all before—there is a natural cycle. No one is panicking just yet." Bryan himself is not going to have to worry about it. He is about to retire.

John Thompson, the engraver, is still working late into the night, though orders have dropped off in the past year. Peter is getting better at signet rings, and the elder Thompson figures his son will be ready to take over the business in two years.

In Halesowen, the old Grove button factory was finally demolished in July 2012, after residents complained that it had become an eyesore. A three-story residential-care home was planned for the site. Peter Grove's button company is managing "to keep our heads above water." Peter hired two new directors, whose expertise is in marketing, and is working to extricate himself from "the heavy responsibility of running and owning the business."

"It is a long haul," he told me, "but in the end it will guarantee the continuance of the business."

As for me, I have become a scrutinizer of suits and overcoats. I exclaimed, no doubt to the annoyance of my family, "Great suit, Wills!," when Prince William appeared on television in a bespoke beauty. I now pay almost as much attention to the cut of George Clooney's tuxedo as I do to his face when I'm flipping through red-carpet magazine reports. In restaurants, I notice the unfortunate way some men's jackets have ridden up behind their necks, and the way others strain at their wearer's midsection. When I spot someone in an overcoat, I zero in on the buttons and find them, almost invariably, wanting.

I have also come to the realization that none of my own clothes really fit me properly. And I have been thinking it would be nice to order myself a bespoke garment someday, if I can ever afford it—a blazer, or maybe even a coat. I'd like to own something beautiful, made by hand, just for me—to know the bliss I heard in the voices of John Cutler's clients when they talked about the way their clothes made them feel.

In the meantime, I am trying to be a better shopper. I haven't sworn off fast fashion, because, let's face it, sometimes the deals are just too amazing. Not long ago, I went to Forever 21 with my seventeen-year-old daughter. She found a truly great back-to-school dress for $12.99. But even in my glee—score!—I am trying to remember the hidden cost of these bargains. And, these days, I do more browsing and less mindless buying.

My dive into bespoke-world got me thinking that these guys, for all their fastidiousness and their foibles, are onto something. I think we could all pay more attention to the materials with which our clothes are made. We could buy fewer things but of better quality. We could search out products made with care and designed to last. We could value the herders, the shearers, the spinners, the weavers, the carvers, and the tailors. We could find beauty in a button. We could be moved, as I was, by the work of many hands to make a single perfect thing.

ACKNOWLEDGMENTS

This book would not have been possible without John Cutler, who welcomed me into his lovely world and guided me through it with patience and élan. I can't begin to thank him. Thanks, too, to Keith Lambert, for being an extraordinarily good sport and for allowing me to peek into his closet.

I am also grateful to the following people, who generously gave me their time, expert advice, and hospitality. In England: Peter Grove, Bryan Dolley, Gary Eastwood, Paul Holt, Alan Dolley, Mark Henderson, Anda Rowland, John Hitchcock, Johnny Allen, Ray Hammett, Roger Goff, and Andrew Chan. In Peru: Jane Wheeler, Raul Rosadio, and the CONOPA crew. In Italy: Stefano Ricci, Filippo Ricci, Claudia Ricci, Niccolò Ricci, Elisa Panzeri, and Douha Ahdab. In Paris: Frédéric Dormeuil and Anne-Sophie de Boissard. In Sydney: Karl Sussmann, Leng Ngo, Genaro Scura, Rhys Twist, David Skillman, Cherelyn Suzuki, Tony Wain, Michael Egan, Tony Canvin, Davis Blumentals, Philip Knowles, Leo Schofield, Bruce Stannard, Nicholas Whitlam, John Thompson, and Peter Thompson. Special thanks to Craig Dyer for being such a gracious host.

Many people went out of their way to help me track down sources and details. Among them were Marti Devore, Leonard

Freedman, Angus Cundey, David Walters, Richard Anderson, Ben Glazier, Brian Lishak, Michael Day, Nigel Birch, Gavin Davis, Anna Lawrence Pietroni, Jenny Swindells, Jocelyn Howells, Robin Larner, Jerry DeHay, Phyllis Culp, Susan Calkins, Mia Hutchinson, Jenny Houldsworth, Annika Trimble, Sharon Katz, Carol Kerven, Sue Wittcutt, Jim Austin, Lulu Skidmore, Gabriela Lichtenstein, Letizia Caimi, Dario Donnini, and Richard D'Aveni. Thank you, all.

David Gould read portions of the book and offered his eloquent and much appreciated encouragement. I'm sure Mrs. Manahan is smiling. Susan Roy also read early drafts and was generous with her astute publishing and fashion advice. Terry Moffatt, as always, cheered me on. Joni B. Cole, Marjorie Mathews, and all the good folks at the Writer's Center in White River Junction, Vermont, gave me guidance and kept me on track. Sam and Joanne Lukens read much of the manuscript and assured me that they would have liked it even if they weren't my parents. T. Alan Broughton inspired me, way back when, to think of myself as a writer. My sincere thanks to them all.

I am forever indebted to my terrific agent, Deborah Grosvenor, of the Grosvenor Literary Agency, first for thinking that a book about an overcoat was a pretty good idea, and then for helping me shape it into something worthy of its home at Spiegel & Grau. I am also extremely grateful to Julie Grau and Hana Landes, my warm, wonderful, and wise editors. I don't know how I got so lucky. Thanks to the rest of the Spiegel & Grau team, including Carol Anderson, Evan Camfield, and Laura Van der Veer, for taking such good care of me.

Thank you to my sister, Andrea, and to Suse, Leslie, Amy, Betsy, Cathie, Karin, Scooter, Wende, and the G3 gang for providing timely and much needed diversions.

Finally, my deepest thanks go to my husband, Michael, and my daughters, Kelley and Claudia, who put up with my absences, both physical and mental, and were there with love, good cheer, and, often, spaghetti carbonara when I returned. I couldn't have done it without them.

NOTES

ix **"One should either be a work"**: Oscar Wilde, "Phrases and Philosophies for the Use of the Young," *The Chameleon*, 1894.

ix **"The woolen-coat"**: Adam Smith, *The Wealth of Nations*, vol. 1, 6th ed., Introduction by Ernest Belfort Bax (London and New York: George Bell & Sons, 1908), p. 12.

INTRODUCTION

xvi **When did clothes become disposable?** Ferdows, Kasra, Michael A. Lewis, and Jose A. D. Machuca, "Rapid-Fire Fulfillment," *Harvard Business Review* 82, no. 11, November 2004.

xix **"Finally, I went to the craftsmen"**: Plato, *Five Dialogues*, trans. George Maximillian Anthony Grube (Indianapolis: Hackett Publishing, 2002), p. 27.

1. THE ROOTS

9 **"I hold that gentleman to be"**: Anthony Trollope, *Thackeray* (London: Macmillan, 1879), p. 200.

11 **Mick and Bianca Jagger:** James Sheridan, *Bespoke: The Men's Style of Savile Row* (New York: Rizzoli, 2010), p. 208.

13 **"It happened quickly"**: Richard Walker, *The Savile Row Story: An Illustrated History* (New York: Prion Books, 1988), p. 17.

14 **"The perfect man, as conceived by"**: Anne Hollander, *Sex and Suits: The Evolution of Modern Dress* (New York: Alfred A. Knopf, 1994), p. 92.

14 **The poster boy for this neoclassic:** Ian Kelly, *Beau Brummell: The Ultimate Man of Style* (New York: Simon & Schuster, 2006).

15 **"Who's your fat friend?"** William Jesse, *The Life of George Brummell, Esq., Commonly Called Beau Brummell* (London: Saunders & Otley, 1844), p. 391.

15 **The essayist Leigh Hunt was imprisoned:** Leigh Hunt, *The Examiner*, London, March 12, 1812.

16 **Lord Byron observed that there were three:** Jesse, *The Life of George Brummell*, p. 15.

16 **Brummell fascinated Virginia Woolf:** Virginia Woolf, *The Second Common Reader: Annotated Version* (Boston: Houghton Mifflin Harcourt, 2003), p. 149.

16 **"His excellence was entirely personal":** Hollander, *Sex and Suits*, p. 9.

19 **Sherman McCoy, the protagonist:** Tom Wolfe, *The Bonfire of the Vanities* (New York: Farrar, Straus & Giroux, 1987), p. 93.

23 **"People who are going to go":** Andy Hawke, "Gieves & Hawkes Exclusive!" *British GQ*, April 25, 2011.

25 **"In actual fact," Hitchcock said:** "Love Thy Neighbour," Savile Row, BBC 4, Episode One, Part 2, first aired February 4, 2008.

26 **"a trap for men":** "A Tailored Trap for Men," *Life*, October 10, 1955, pp. 126–30. .

26 **The Armani look also bridged:** Woody Hochswender, "Review/Fashion: Images of Man, Labeled Armani," *The New York Times*, December 21, 1990.

26 **It didn't help that the era's:** Clover Hope, "The 15 Worst Dressed Men of Silicon Valley," *GQ*, August 3, 2011.

29 **Looking at the popularity:** Shira Ovide, "Perfect Fit: To Some Outfits, Nothing Speaks Like 'Bespoke,'" *The Wall Street Journal*, May 3, 2012.

30 **"It's like Build-A-Bear":** E. Palmieri and Brenner Thomas, "From Savile Row to Main Street: Custom Suits Go Mass," *Women's Wear Daily*, March 11, 2010.

30 **Tailor Made's website acknowledged:** www.tailormadelondon.com.

32 **"Mass luxury is not luxury at all":** "Made to Treasure," *South China Morning Post*, June 17, 2011.

33 **Global Blue, a retail-market-research:** Simon O'Connell, "The Growing Complexity of the Chinese Shopper," www.luxurysociety.com, April 13, 2012.

2. THE FLEECE

41 **"What is this strange animal"**: Sylvan Stroock, *Vicuña: The World's Finest Fabric* (New York: S. Stroock, 1937), p. 7.

45 **As early as 1553:** Pedro Cieza de León, *The Incas*, ed. Victor Wolfgang Von Hagen, trans. Harriet De Onis (Norman: University of Oklahoma Press, 1959).

45 **"Such in those times was"**: Garcilaso de la Vega, *First Part of the Royal Commentaries of the Incas*, vol. 2, trans. Sir Paul Rycaut (London: M. Flesher, 1688), p. 195.

46 **In 1768, viceroy Marqués:** Luis J. Cueto and Carlos F. Ponce, *Management of Vicuña: Its Contribution to Rural Development in the High Andes of Peru* (Rome: Food & Agriculture Organization of the United Nations, 1985), p. 3.

47 **"Yes, rare indeed is the vicuna"**: Stroock, *Vicuna: The World's Finest Fabric*.

47 **At Christmastime in 1938:** "Manufacturing: Stroock's Fleece," *Time*, January 2, 1939.

47 **"As long as the lady is"**: Charles Brackett, Billy Wilder, and D. M. Marshman, Jr., *Sunset Boulevard* script, dated March 21, 1949.

48 **Stanley Marcus, the former chairman:** Stanley Marcus, *Minding the Store* (Denton: University of North Texas Press, 1974) p. 190.

48 **In 1955, *Life* magazine reported:** "Glad Tidings About Glad Rags," *Life*, July 11, 1955.

48 **In 1957, Jack Kerouac wore an:** Ellis Amburn, *Subterranean Kerouac: The Hidden Life of Jack Kerouac* (New York: St. Martin's Press, 1998), p. 262.

48 **That same year, the slugger Ted Williams:** Tom Fitzgerald, "Open Season," *San Francisco Chronicle*, July 8, 2002.

49 **"I began to bellow and shout"**: Faith McNulty, "Peruvian Conservationist," *The New Yorker*, October 4, 1976.

3. THE LINING

75 **It didn't hurt that:** Nicola White, *Reconstructing Italian Fashion: America and the Development of the Italian Fashion Industry* (Oxford and New York: Berg, 2000), p. 38.

82 **According to Confucius, the story:** *Silk, Mohair, Cashmere and Other Luxury Fabrics*, ed. Robert R. Franck (Cambridge, England: Woodhead Publishing, and Boca Raton, Florida: CRC Press, 2001).

83 **In 2011, researchers from England:** Tom Gheysens et al., "Demineralization Enables Reeling of Wild Silkmoth Cocoons," *Biomacromolecules* 12, no. 6 (2011): 2257–66.

86 **In the past two decades:** Peter S. Goodman, "China's Silk Noose Tightens," *The Washington Post*, December 18, 2003.

87 **In one case, the Babei Textile Company:** James Kynge, *China Shakes the World* (New York: Houghton Mifflin Harcourt, 2006) p. 88.

87 **With the production rate:** Guy Dinmore, "Tuscan Town Turns Against Chinese Migrants," *Financial Times*, February 8, 2010.

87 **What seemed to annoy some Italians:** Rachel Donadio, "Chinese Remake the 'Made in Italy' Fashion Label," *The New York Times*, September 12, 2010.

94 **The conversation makes me think:** Mary McCarthy, *The Stones of Florence* (New York: Harcourt, Brace, 1959), p. 4.

4. THE MERCHANT

103 **"I pity the man":** Benjamin Harrison, *Speeches of Benjamin Harrison, Twenty-third President of the United States,* compiled by Charles Hedges (New York: United States Book Company, 1892), p. 548.

117 **Researchers from University College Dublin:** Browne, Mark et al., 2011. "Accumulation of Microplastic on Shorelines Worldwide: Sources and Sinks," *Environmental Science and Technology* 45, no. 21 (2011): 9175–79.

5. THE CLOTH

130 **As Charlotte Brontë wrote:** Charlotte Brontë, *Shirley: A Tale* (London: Smith, Elder, 1849), p. 39.

130 **"What loomed before them":** Kirkpatrick Sale, *Rebels Against the Future: The Luddites and Their War on the Industrial Revolution* (Boston: Addison-Wesley, 1995), p. 8.

131 **"Besides taking the children":** John Ramsay McCulloch, *A Statistical Account of the British Empire,* vol. 2 (London: Charles Knight, 1837), p. 86.

131 **"Cooped up in a heated atmosphere":** P. Gaskell, *The Manufacturing Population of England* (London: Baldwin & Cradock, 1833), p. 202.

132 **"It is too late now":** Charles Wing, *Evils of the Factory System Demonstrated by Parliamentary Evidence* (London: Frank Cass, 1837), p. 28.

134 **"Here . . . in the Huddersfields":** James Morris, *The Road to Huddersfield: A Journey to Five Continents* (New York: Pantheon Books, 1963), p. 4.

135 **"Cumbersome baggage will be":** Harland Manchester, "New Suits Stay Pressed All Summer," *Popular Science*, April 1952.

139 **And there was the disheartening:** *Crap Towns: The 50 Worst Places to Live in the UK*, ed. Sam Jordison and Dan Kieran (London: Boxtree, 2003).

6. THE BUTTONS

149 **"It is wonderful, is it not?"** Charles Dickens, "What There Is in a Button," *Household Words*, April 10, 1852.

150 **"The men, women, children, country":** Cecil Woodham-Smith, *Queen Victoria: Her Life and Times, 1819–1861*, vol. 1 (London: Cardinal, 1975), p. 119.

150 **In The Old Curiosity Shop:** Charles Dickens, *The Old Curiosity Shop* (Hertfordshire, U.K.: Wordsworth Classics, 1995), p. 44.

153 **"Buttonholes! There is something lively":** Laurence Sterne, *The Life and Opinions of Tristram Shandy, Gentleman* (London: James Cochrane, 1832), p. 270.

154 **White wrote that the development:** Lynn T. White, *Medieval Religion and Technology: Collected Essays* (Berkeley, Los Angeles, and London: University of California Press, 1978), p. 273.

155 **It was a new social order:** Diane Epstein and Millicent Safro, *Buttons* (New York: Harry N. Abrams, 1991), p. 25.

156 **In fifteenth-century London:** *English Medieval Industries: Crafts, Techniques, Products*, ed. Blair and Nigel Ramsay (London and Rio Grande, Ohio: Hambledon Press, 1991), p. 373.

156 **This, despite the fact:** R. Campbell, *The London Tradesman: Being a Compendious View of All the Trades, Professions, Arts, Both Liberal and Mechanic, Now Practiced in the Cities of London and Westminster* (London: T. Gardner, 1747), p. 245.

164 **"Buttons turned out to be":** Nicholas Kristof, "Qiaotou Journal: Chinese Bet Their Shirts on Buttons and, Bingo!" *The New York Times*, January 18, 1993.

166 **"The set was the scorecard":** Steven M. Gelber, *Hobbies: Leisure and the Culture of Work in America* (New York: Columbia University Press, 1999), p. 76

166 **"It was not uncommon while":** *The American Archaeologist*, vols. 2–3 (Columbus, Ohio: Landon Printing & Publishing, 1898), p. 332.

167 **The show, called Hobby Lobby:** Gelber, *Hobbies*, p. 47.

167 **"become more charming and beautiful":** "Do Men Have the Most Fun?" *Ladies' Home Journal,* October 1939.

167 **"Nearly two thirds of buttons":** Lillian Smith Albert and Kathryn Schwerke, *The Complete Button Book* (Garden City, N.Y.: Doubleday, 1949), p. viii.

167 **"The absurdity of collecting":** Gelber, *Hobbies,* p. 64.

168 **"Buttons are the fossils":** *The World According to Martha,* ed. Bill Adler (New York: McGraw-Hill, 2005), p. 52.

169 **Simon Doonan, creative director:** Simon Doonan, "Shoplifting Retailers Chase Hightailers: Fleece Is Very In This Fall," *The New York Observer,* September 29, 2003.

170 **An 1892 issue of:** *Chemist + Druggist,* vol. 40, March 5, 1892, p. 345.

7. THE GOLD TRIMMINGS

179 **"When a work lifts your spirits":** Jean de la Bruyère, *The Characters of Jean de la Bruyère* (London: John C. Nimmo, 1885), p. 18.

184 **"The steadiness of nerve":** "Spokane Engraver Cuts Prayer on Head of Pin, Monogram on Needle Point," *The Spokesman-Review,* Spokane, Wash.: February 21, 1915.

8. THE TAILOR

191 **"A smack of all Human Life lies":** Thomas Carlyle, *The Works of Thomas Carlyle: Past and Present* (New York: Peter Fenelon Collier, 1897), p. 424.

200 **"Eventually, though, the pressure":** Robert Ross, *Clothing: A Global History* (Cambridge, Mass.: Polity Press, 2008), p. 170.

201 **"They wear shiny frock-coats":** R.E.N. Twopenny, *Town Life in Australia* (London: Elliot Stock, 1883), p. 79.

202 **"I was always given a chair":** Lydia Gill, *My Town: Sydney in the 1930's* (Sydney: State Library of NSW Press, 1993).

9. THE COAT

223 **"Costly thy habit as thy purse":** William Shakespeare, *Hamlet,* Act 1, Scene 3, 70–72.

EPILOGUE

229 **"Those who find beautiful meanings":** Oscar Wilde, *The Picture of Dorian Gray* (Oxford, U.K.: Oxford University Press, 1981), p. xxiii.

ABOUT THE AUTHOR

Meg Lukens Noonan has written for many publications, including *Outside, National Geographic Adventure, Travel + Leisure, Esquire, Men's Journal,* and *The New York Times.* She lives in New Hampshire with her husband and two daughters.

ABOUT THE TYPE

This book was set in Goudy Old Style, a type-
face designed by Frederic William Goudy (1865–
1947). Goudy began his career as a bookkeeper,
but devoted the rest of his life in pursuit of "recognized quality" in a printing type.

Goudy Old Style was produced in 1914 and
was an instant bestseller for the foundry. It has
generous curves and smooth, even color. It is re-
garded as one of Goudy's finest achievements.